Bodies, Bou
Delight:

A 3-Step empowerment system
for parents and professionals of children aged 0-5

Written by Julia Saunders, MEd

Dear Kerri

Thanks for all
you do!
see the best.

Juli

Bodies, Boundaries & Delight:

A 3-Step empowerment system
for parents and professionals of children aged 0-5

Step 1: Talk about bodies.

Step 2: Teach boundaries and consent.

Step 3: Encourage curiosity and delight.

Written by Julia Saunders, MEd

Table of Contents

BBD Step 1: Talking About Bodies
Ages Four to Five
Great Observers, Terrible Interpreters
Talking 'Sexy'
Simple Examples
Self-Reflection Exercise

BBD Step 2: Teach Boundaries and Consent
Boundary Intelligence
Emotional Intelligence
Self-Reflection exercise
Personal Space and Boundaries
Their Body is Their Own
What's Private and What's Public
The Mind Body Connection
Peer Pressure Starts Early
Media Savvy Parenting

BBD Step 2: Teach Boundaries and Consent
Ages Birth to One
Simple Examples

BBD Step 2: Teach Boundaries and Consent
Ages One to Two
Practice Teaching about Private Parts
Two Loops of Arousal
Simple Examples

BBD Step 2: Teach Boundaries and Consent
Ages Two to Three
Good Touch/Bad Touch
Emotional Education and Intuition
Your Body is Your Own
Self-Reflection Exercise
Simple Porn Proofing Strategies for your Preschooler

Acknowledgements

To Jamie, my beloved husband and partner. Without you there would be no possibility of this book being written. How could I ever thank you enough? Your unending faith, hard work, and keeping us afloat with your humour and wisdom – you helped make this book a reality, for the benefit of all who read it.

To my three wee children, for a richness of examples that fill these pages with the truth and reality of 'what is'. Thanks to you also for your patience with Mumma as I've been working hard these past few months and having less for you all.

To all the generous supporters of me and my work. When I needed that boost, there you were to light the fire under me. I trust you know who you are – so much gratitude!

Introduction: Why Knowing is Better

Our Sexual Spirit

Over the past 16 years, in my practice as a sexual health educator and trainer, and in recent years as a coach specializing in family life, sex and relationship, I began to see patterns in clients', students', and professionals' struggles. Where did these patterns come from and why? As I have been unraveling the emotional, mental, social, and physiological interplay that sexuality has on a person's body and mind, I've discovered what seems to be a universal struggle. Most people have some kind of innate shame and low self-esteem around their sexuality, and sexual expression, which tends to play out in their life through struggles to be authentic, to feel fulfilled or to find what they are seeking.

This book is my answer to changing the tides of these generationally ingrained patterns, to inspire and heal parts of our sexual self-esteem, and to guide and inform so we may positively affect those most intimately engaged in our life – our children. You see, it is from the very beginning that our sexual spirit unfolds. Parental influence is by far the most meaningful and has the most lasting impression on our psyche. The way we are raised builds the foundation for our very existence, in every capacity, and of course, no less, our sexuality.

No pressure, right?

Where **did** all this culture of shaming our body and spirit's natural desires and delights come from? For hundreds of years many cultures have demonized the body and its sexual expression. Our parents certainly weren't the first to be enculturated to believe these things. If we dive into the history of sexuality we find a rabbit hole of social control – through shaming and shutting down what is natural and healthy for most of us. Our parents are not to blame and neither are we. Most of us were raised 'in the dark', and without proper factual knowledge, so we assumed this whole body and sex thing was naturally a place of embarrassment and secrecy.

Our history has been perpetuated into the present. When I had my first child it became crystal clear to me that I was stumped, confused and afraid to discuss the topic. Yes, me, the professional sexual health educator! I felt awkward using appropriate body science terminology, especially in front of others. Even though I was educationally equipped with complete comfort in the subject area **and** had tons of information in my knowledge base about 'age appropriate sex ed' and how to 'best deliver it', I felt uncomfortable and could not do it effectively with my young child!

Feelings of **my** sexual shame and low self-esteem coloured the way I spoke to my daughter. What I thought about and how I experienced her growing body and sexual expressions caused strong emotional reactions within me. I also struggled with embarrassment or negativity from people in my life when I started talking about children's body parts or boundaries, toileting, pregnancy, birth or other related subjects. My awkwardness was even more pronounced when I spoke to my daughter. I began to feel oppressed and questioned when and how to start this whole huge topic with little kids? If _I_ struggled so much, what did that say about society in general – and how could I help?

I have lived in the same city in Canada for 47 years and am actually third generation here. I mention this because this book and its ideas are very 'North American Centric'. As a reader you may struggle to find your culture, ethnicity, and/or values in my writing. That said, my lens **seems** to be the dominant one in media, which is heavily consumed around the globe. As media is **the** biggest teacher of sexuality - outside our closest inner circle of family, and peers - I hope that the messages within this book will be helpful to all cultures and value systems. I invite you to sculpt this 3-Step system to best fit your family or the children you influence.

Sex, Body and Boundary Education are key pieces of the large and complex puzzle of a healthy whole self. Interestingly however, is the huge lack of knowledge and education throughout the entire system of North American society (and I would offer most of the rest of the world). There is a huge gap in needed sex education – ranging from baby and birth preparation books and classes, parent education, and professional development training (such as for early childhood education). There is a total lack of sexual health training for a variety of professionals who teach in our communities. The situation in our elementary and secondary school systems is inadequate, at best, including a total lack of teacher education and the official curriculum having 'too little, too late' for all children and teens in the system. We are not in a good place and are not keeping up.

A lack of standardized materials and reliable, accurate information available to parents to educate themselves and their children about sexuality and sexual health is part of what feeds the problems in our culture. Research pumps out stats on STI's, unplanned pregnancies, complaints from young people about how much they want sex ed and don't get it, terribly disturbing stats on relationship abuse, sexual harassment and rape – the list goes on. Social media is rife with examples of complete lack of knowledge of the most basic bodily structures, functions, and more importantly of information on boundaries and consent.

This lack of comprehensive sex and relationship education, woven throughout the very structure of society, is part of what holds us in ignorance, shame and secrecy. Although this ingrained shame and secrecy is part of what prevents change, I feel a tide of change is upon us. We are at a breaking point and I believe this book will be the foundation parents and professionals need to truly change that tide. You may be picking this up when your children are grown but all change starts with us. You **can** be that pioneer that supports others in educating and developing themselves out of the darkness we are in.

Sex Education begins at home, from the very start, whether or not we ever say or do a thing to *consciously* teach the subject. In my professional development trainings or parent education classes I experience participants who share stories of how silence teaches. What is **not** said can have a profound effect on imprinting our thinking and how we make sense of the world. I hear examples of how their parents shut down questions or curiosities, or how they received a book when they were well into (or almost out) of puberty. As we have learned, this type of sex ed is too little, too late, but our parents' generation didn't have the knowledge, or the tools, to do things any differently so how can we be surprised?

Why Knowing is Better

Most people who fight against comprehensive sex education believe that the innocence of children must be protected. I have heard "Above all else, let them grow up first before they must be burdened with such things". The fear behind this statement comes from a place of ingrained embarrassment and secrecy and serves as an example of how society oppresses and is oppressed by the historical shame of sexuality. It is not easy to fight against what indoctrinates society but we can no longer turn a blind eye. Can we?

There are many reasons to talk to our little ones about bodies and sexuality - from birth. Early childhood sex education is primarily about Health, Science and Safety (in the words of Meg Hickling, preeminent sex educator in Canada). Not only does talking about sexual health, body science and safety help caregivers and parents to develop a bond and keep children safe, it supports the development of a safe haven. Here they can come and ask questions about themselves as the world around them becomes more and more complex.

Can we imagine how important it will be when our young child or teen feels most comfortable coming to us as a trusted adult because we have worked to build this bond of trust? We will be confident to answer their questions in line with **our** values and ideas, not someone else's (or worse yet their peers or the media!)

One of **the** most important reasons to talk about these topics is that children educated and knowledgeable in the areas of human sexuality and boundaries are **abuse resistant**. Hands down one of the key outcomes of comprehensive sexual health information, across the early lifespan and continuing into teenage hood, is an abuse and bully-protected child. We work to equip them with knowledge about their bodies, what is private and what is to be respected about themselves and others. In doing this, we help protect everyone both emotionally and physically.

Children equipped with sexual health information, starting with simple, basic 'body science' and building on their knowledge base about this very complex and interwoven topic over time, are equipped to navigate safely through the world around them, both online and off. *Boundaries and Delight* education empowers children to **enjoy** themselves and thereby increases their self-esteem, guiding them to have an enriched experience of themselves and their body. This power can be instrumental in a persons' overall well-being – across their lifespan. My purpose here is that our children have the tools and knowledge to protect themselves when we are no longer as nearby, but also that they possess **the capacity** to know themselves deeply and, most importantly, are able to ask for what they want in life in a safer and consensual way.

You may be familiar with some threats to children's sexual and personal safety: bullies, abusers, and predators, whether peers, strangers, in our communities or through the internet. You may know that most sexual misconduct occurs from known persons such as friends and family members. I've personally heard many that have happened because of siblings or cousins who took advantage. But, have you considered that these threats can also mean absorbing harmful messages from the media or from peers - both younger and older? As children grow more and more independent, they are freer to wreak havoc on each other, unwitnessed by the watchful eyes of caring adults. In this day and age, all people need more knowledge and power to protect themselves. This crucial process of learning begins at home, with you.

Sexuality across the Lifespan
Sexuality can be seen as fluid and ever-changing across our lifetime. We are open to influence from many sources and that usually

continues through life. It is very natural and healthy to experiment and explore our body from very early on, as young as 18 months or 2 or 3 years old. This can continue throughout our lifetime. That said, some refrain from exploring their sexuality or the sexuality of others, while others simply aren't inspired to be sexual, either in their youth, or as they live out their lives. Whether active or not, sexuality is a part of **all** of us, from birth to death, and understanding something so basic and human would seem only natural.

We live in our bodies from conception to death and so it would seem to make sense to know a lot about ours and others, wouldn't it? Why **is** it such a difficult and scary thing to talk and learn about? I truly believe that it is our generationally ingrained fear, shame, and lack of open education that keeps our mouths and hearts shut. So, then, how do we find it **within** to break these chains and change the potentiality of our children's lives? How can we grow from where we are now? How can we heal or reconcile what is inside so we pass on to our children what we truly wish to pass on - and not the rest? How can we talk differently to our children so they can truly benefit from our learnings?

Be encouraged that such a huge and complex topic must be taught slowly, over time. I recommend following the steps in this guide:

beginning with simple body science and enjoyment, building on our ability to talk about more complex areas, such as boundaries and consent, over time. Eventually we will be able to spark conversations on more intricate and positive aspects of sexuality with our child, such as the feelings of being loved, pleasure, respect, knowing our body and what it likes, gender, consent and sexual diversity.

Why So Early in a Child's Life?

All very young children are at a stage in their development that makes them excited about almost anything, especially if it is presented in a positive way. They take information given to them quite matter-of-factly – without shame, guilt, or often even questioning the messenger (that comes later!). The more comfortable they are with body science, boundaries, consent and healthy sexuality, the more the conversations will be comfortable for them to talk about as they grow. This is protective on many levels. Eventually, the more a young person knows about the whole picture the more they will delay sexual activities that may harm them, i.e. early intercourse or pornography use.

What I've learned, based on years of researching, giving parent education and professional development classes, writing, as well as coaching in my practice, is that many, if not most, parents hold some type of sexual trauma, shame or guilt about their body and/or their sexuality. They may have sustained sexual abuse or molestation from family or others, or experienced peers or media teaching oppressive concepts that they internalized as true. Some of us simply lived on misinformation. All of these scenarios can lead to a less than positive sexual footing. In my workshops, many parents tell disturbing tales about their path to understanding themselves and having a healthy sexuality. Some begin to see where they are maligned and misinformed. Many are full of fear they will pass on negative views, attitudes or opinions to their little ones.

Often, because of a parent's fears, negativity or oppression uncomfortable topics never get brought up with their child. Some parents avoiding topics to do with bodies and sexuality, others may use 'cute' euphemisms like 'Pee Pee' for penis, or 'V-J-J', for vulva, and then send a book their child's way once they are well into puberty. This is a dangerous practice, unfortunately. Our child may never come to us with issues, questions, or anything else in the realm of sexuality, because we never brought it to attention. Some kids naturally never ask. Usually young people from these types of situations end up going to their peers or the internet to learn what they want to know and there could be **no worse place** to start becoming informed about something as crucial to our healthy 'whole self' as our sexuality.

I don't mean to scare but rather to impress on the importance of **us**, as the parent or caregiver, to work through our issues of fear, shame, guilt, and our own misinformation, by becoming educated, using the tools and resources in this book and transforming into a Trusted Adult. It takes practice, and lots of it, to effectively talk and teach about *Bodies, Boundaries and Delight*. It often also takes finding support to help unlock our blocks and traumas through methods like coaching and counselling. Our lives can be changed if we want them to be. Releasing these binds on our body image, sexuality, boundaries and ability to delight in ourselves and others can truly bring us a kind of freedom and pleasure in life that we may rarely (or never) have experienced.

One thing I haven't mentioned yet is how crucial it is that sex education comes **before** we actually need the information and understanding. Problem is, this idea flies in the face of what most of society **believes**. But, it is true on every level and is well supported in research – our children need information, comprehension and tools in advance of ever actually using them, to best be prepared to handle the ravages of the social world.

Let me leave you with this: can you imagine if we had been equipped with this complex knowledge well before puberty started, how our experience of puberty would have been radically different? That this period of our life could have been explored with curiosity and delight, with little or no shame and with strong boundaries against what we did or did not want to do? How would that have changed our lives completely?

We begin, then, to protect **and** empower our children by equipping them with knowledge about theirs and others bodies, teaching them skills on how to develop and clearly communicate their boundaries, and helping them to build their self-esteem and confidence in the face of anything. Education is power and by giving them the confidence and knowledge they need to speak out about and protect themselves, we equip them with life skills that will serve them their entire lives.

Children rely on us to guide them through all aspects of life, until they can find their own way. If we care enough to be their guide and mentor through life, respecting them and considering their whole self, we can literally change the world. Through even that one child you reach they, in turn, will make a difference in their life and the relationships around them.

How to Use this Book and the Resources

My intention with this guidebook is two-fold: a resource for those who are seeking reliable, dependable, age appropriate sex education for their children aged 0-5 (and up), and a workbook of sorts, for you as a parent or professional to reflect on your own sexual oppression and other aspects that may ail your sexuality and sexual expression. This guidebook may seem 'too advanced' for some, and 'yes, I already knew that' for others but my intention, like in my sex ed classes, is to speak to the middle. I am confident you will find yourself in this book no matter where you stand on the issues within it.

I use the term 'parent' universally throughout the book, often I mention Professionals, and sometimes Trusted Adults. A Trusted Adult refers to any type of parent, guardian, or an ethical adult who works with children, or an adult that a child trusts for guidance and support, including professionals.

Our efforts towards our children happens every minute we are in their presence and very often when we aren't with them. We already talk about bodies every day. We give limits to our children constantly and help them to navigate boundaries and consent every day. We delight in our children and support their exploration in multiple ways. This book guides parents to do these things within the realm of bodies, sexuality, gender and some other typically taboo 'topics'.

Guidelines:

- Seek to explore your feelings, values, thoughts, and beliefs about the Steps and why you may have them.
- Become clear on what you want to share with your child on the topics, or not, and why, or why not.
- As you review and become familiar with appropriate, research-based knowledge for the age and/or stage of your children you may notice that my lists are about two years younger. This is important as everything is backing up in time with what children are learning and being exposed to.
- Although I recommend keeping up with the research you do not have to do each step as the ages suggest. You can decide what you want to share now and what you are going to leave behind for now. It is a good idea to also reflect on why.
- Using the lists of resources for each topic area, feel free to read further about the topics you are most interested in or feel especially challenged by. The list of resources at the end of the book is extensive.
- Use the examples in this book if you want a script for those particularly challenging areas and have fun creating your own

versions. Any examples given in the previous age are also good to use moving up the ages.

- You will be delighted (and maybe freaked out) by what your children ask and talk about. Journal about how it goes, any questions your child comes back to you with and feelings that come up for you. Note down how you responded, or didn't.

- Talk and share with your children about your experiences and feelings. Ask them questions about theirs. Consider what you would have liked your parents to have said to you at (insert age).

- It is ideal to have conversations about bodies, boundaries and sexuality/sensuality at home, where we are more comfortable and there are few distractions, but no matter where or when they ask questions it's a good rule of thumb to respond with **"That's a good question!"** (giving kudos to Meg Hickling for this rule). Follow this response with "Let's talk about that when we are driving home", "Let's talk about that when we have our bath tonight", etc.

What do I say to the 'non-believers'?

Give some thought on how you are going to describe this practice to those around you who will have influence on and/or exposure to your child. These important people may put up a fight against your intentions to educate your child in this way. You may have to work to coach those around you about the benefits of effective lifespan-based sex ed.

Some of my responses include:

"Part of my intention is to teach children to live and grow without body shame and secrecy, so they can feel empowered and be protected from abusers or the internet."

"The more they know at the right time, the better. It has been heavily researched – start very early."

"I prefer to teach them autonomy over their bodies and their preferences so they feel good about themselves."

"Early body and boundaries education supports their self-esteem and protects them."

"Research states that we start really young and I need the practice so I'm prepared when the questions get harder!"

This is a relatively new and progressive way of approaching 'whole-self sexual health'. The **Bodies, Boundaries & Delight 3-Step System** also makes this complex and potentially challenging area of life a whole lot easier to talk about, protect against, and to ultimately enjoy. You are truly a pioneer for the children in your care and I can guarantee they will be grateful for your courage and forward thinking. Good luck and please be in touch!

Julia @ slieducation.com

BBD Step 1: Talking About Bodies

This work is about us, the parents, first and foremost.

The intention with this very early start is not only to help children become familiar with the topic areas and build on their knowledge over time but more importantly, at this stage, for us as parents to be able to do this in a comfortable way. We begin with the initial use of 'body science' language when dressing, diapering and bathing our newborn and continue this practice in to toddler and preschool age.

Our ability to use correct terminology, when our babies are too young to catch the nuances of any shame or embarrassment we may feel, will serve to build our comfort and competency in a safe way with the subject areas in this book. When we are comfortable, they are comfortable. As a parent or trusted adult in their lives, we are their primary sex educator and how our emotions underwrite our words speaks volumes. Practice, practice, practice until the words are as easy to say as elbows, knees and nose. Our comfort and frequent, relaxed ways of talking about bodies and sexuality will also boost their self-esteem and keep them protected.

BBD Step 1: Talking About Bodies

Ages Birth to One

From the first moments we hold our baby and can find the time to relax with them in private, we can begin talking about their body to them. We can delight in their delicate soft skin, enjoy the smell of them, and slowly, with curiosity, explore all the parts of their bodies while speaking to them about what and where we are touching (you will be getting to know them all quite well over time!). These sacred moments, getting to know our baby and helping them to connect to us and feel safe with us, are just the beginning of this special journey of Sex Education at Home.

Take a look at the list of body parts below. If you are not sure of where these are and what their function is, please see the list of resources at the end of the book and do more study in this area. You might be surprised what you don't know! (A bonus of increasing knowledge about bodies is the potential of changing one's sex life for the better!)

If there is only one children's resource you buy at this time I recommend *It's NOT the Stork*, written by Robie H. Harris. *It's Not the Stork* has a thorough collection of illustrations, by Michael Emberley, which touch on just about every topic discussed in *Bodies, Boundaries & Delight*. This book is labelled 'ages 4 and up' but the illustrations are just fine for showing to our interested 1 to 5 year old. This book works well because our children can't read yet so we can choose what we share with them about the illustrations. Another, more simplistic book that has good illustrations for the under 5 set is *Boys, Girls & Body Science*, by Meg Hickling. Illustrations really help to increase our children's understanding about bodies. If you prefer to use a children's book to teach a topic or Step, rather than having many little conversations, please find some in the Resources at the end of the book.

The following list includes the most basic body science words to be used over and over by age one. These are some of the private body parts that may come up in conversation, either with other caretakers, grandparents, aunts and uncles, etc., while diapering, teaching natural elimination, toilet training, bathing or discussing our babies' body with doctors and other healthcare providers.

Both: **Nipples, Anus, Buttocks, Genitals**

Girls: **Vulva*, Breasts**

Boys: **Penis, Foreskin, Scrotum, Testicles**

*Note: The vulva is the part of the female sexual organs that are on the outside – the parts we can see and touch. The vulva is often wrongly referred to as the 'vagina'. The vagina is a tube that attaches the outside of the body – the vulva, to the inside, the cervix and uterus. During the first year there is no real need to speak about the vagina, clitoris, urethra, labia or hymen at this point, unless you or health care professionals want or need to, of course!

Simple Examples:

"This is your vulva."

"These are your nipples. Most people have nipples. Mummy's are bigger than yours, see?" "These are Mummy's breasts. You will get yours when you are older."

"Daddies nipples are smaller than Mummy's."

"Here is your penis and this is your scrotum."

"The testicles inside your scrotum are very delicate – be gentle."

"Mummy cleans your anus after you have a bowel movement (or whatever word you use in your house, like 'poo')."

"Be gentle with your foreskin. We don't need to pull it back until we are older."

"Buttocks are usually covered by our diaper. It feels nice to sit them in the bath and wash them, doesn't it?

"Our genitals are sensitive so we touch them gently."

BBD Step 2: Talking About Bodies

Ages One to Two

This is the age where we can begin to speak more specifically about their body and other people's bodies. In this year our children begin to understand much of the things we say, especially if we repeat them frequently. The more comfortable we are talking about bodies the more comfortable our children will be. Building our comfort and competency with this area has a very direct effect on how our children will feel about themselves and others. Having comfort with their bodies deeply impacts their self-esteem and their openness (or shame) about themselves and their blooming sensuality and sexuality.

This is the stage where our little ones become more mobile and are able to interact with others in a more determined way. As they express their curiosity we will want to talk about our body, our partners' body and other siblings within the lens of *Step 2: Teach Boundaries and Consent*. It is also important to make a decision for ourselves whether we are comfortable with our child looking at or touching our genitals because it is a very natural curiosity for children under 5. They will also be interested in our toileting and so it is important to reflect on how we feel about this and why. Consider how we might want our children to have a different or similar experience than we did as a child and how to make that a reality for them at this stage.

The following are basic body science words to be shared and understood by age two. While diapering, teaching natural elimination, toilet training, bathing or discussing our child's body with doctors and other healthcare providers, these are some basic sexual body parts that may come up in conversation. It is important that all caretakers are familiar with the fact that we choose to use scientific words so the message can be as consistent as possible. Even if we don't use them all the time it will be important for our young child to be familiar with the scientific terms.

Both: **Nipples, Anus, Buttocks, Genitals**

Girls: **Vulva, Clitoris, Vagina, Breasts**

Boys: **Penis, Foreskin, Scrotum, Testicles**

Simple Examples: We can use examples from the previous age at any time.
"Everyone has genitals on the outside of their body. Girls (usually) have a vulva and boys (usually) have a penis and scrotum with testicles in it."
"(most) Girls have lots more (sexual body parts) on the inside."
"Did you want to take a look at a picture of what's inside?"

"Your vulva helps protect your clitoris and vagina.... keeping your delicate body parts clean and safe."

"It's a good thing we have buttocks. Our buttocks help protect our anus and genitals when we sit or when we fall."

"We wash our hands before and after touching our genitals. This keeps us and others clean and protected (i.e. from germs)."

"I can see you are holding your vulva/genitals/penis/scrotum. Do you need to pee?"

"Yes, that is urine in the toilet/in your diaper. Most people call it pee."

"I can smell a fart, sweetie. Do you need to have a bowel movement (BM)/ take a poop?"

BBD Step 1: Talking About Bodies

Ages Two to Three

Please review the information in the section above as it pertains to this age as well. Before our little ones turn two we probably experience them as very curious - about everything. By the time they are three (preschoolers) they may be asking questions that are increasingly challenging to answer. As we have already laid down the basic body science foundation in the first two years these more difficult subjects won't hit so hard.

Introducing 'Sex'

It may seem surprising that we see words like sex and erections at this early age but they are already being exposed to them! Not only is society becoming more open about where babies come from (and what sex is), media dictates our reality more and more, and our children, as young as three, are absorbing these messages. Many are starting to ask questions.

Although some children may never ask questions it is important to have body science discussions while they are openly curious and want to know basic human things, such as how babies are made and how do they get here? Children this age do not harbor body shame and are very easy to teach. It also really helps us, as the adults, to increase our comfort by talking and teaching about these most basic human behaviours while our toddler is still too young to internalize the embarrassment we may feel.

Sometime before our child reaches five it will be important to begin the discussion about what 'sex' is. Some families may begin this around age 3. A lot of what we share may go over their heads but the art of practicing is helpful. As we become more comfortable and knowledgeable about bodies and sexuality we naturally soften and open to our children around the subject. This softening is read by our children and they can relax about it too. Answer their questions as they arise and don't worry about telling them 'too much'. They will absorb what they are interested in and the rest will be forgotten, for now.

The book *Sex is a Funny Word: A Book about Bodies, Feelings, and YOU*, by Cory Silverberg, is a great resource to help any trusted adult to find multiple ways to talk about this complex and value-ridden subject. This book is available in the library, is very open to interpretation and works well for children over 5 years. My eldest, at the age of 7, read it in an hour and said "It helped put lots of pieces together for me". I'm assuming these pieces are the ones I've been busily putting in her head over the years because, no, she didn't have any questions. (Lol!)

If we don't feel comfortable talking about sex for pleasure (although this is one of the main reasons people do it), we can start by saying something like "Many people have sex to make babies, when they are older". This is a true statement, albeit a small piece of the picture, but it is honest and we can always build on this information as they mature and ask more questions.

Being prepared will continue to be an important factor if we want to be their trusted adult. Reading up on books such as *Sex is a Funny Word* ahead of time is very supportive of us on our path. Having trusted adults in their lives, adults who they can ask any question to, is a vital aspect of keeping children safe, as well as protecting their self-esteem and security.

The following list includes the most basic body science words to be shared and understood by age three. These are the parts of the human body and systems that tend to come up when seeing a pregnant woman or a new baby, conversations with caretakers, grandparents, aunts and uncles, etc., while diapering, toilet training, bathing or in discussions with doctors and other healthcare providers.

Both:	**Nipples, Anus, Buttocks, Genitals, Urethra (or Urethral opening), Sex, Erections, Urine, Stool**
Girls:	**Vulva, Labia, Clitoris, Vagina, Breasts, Uterus, Ovum**
Boys:	**Penis, Foreskin, Scrotum, Testicles, Sperm**

Even if we don't use the technical terms consistently it will be important for our young child to be familiar with them. Being straightforward with terms of body science will help them understand it is a natural and normal part of being human and talking about it in your family is okay. We can remind them that having these types of discussion in private is always a good idea as we are talking about private body parts.

Please remember that we can always put our particular cultures' or family's values into the teaching as we see appropriate. For example, when talking about why people have sex we can state whatever reason we want our children to believe and follow. Remember, though, that they will eventually learn the truth. Being as truthful and direct as possible will help build the trust and close relationship we want with our children well into their future and young adulthood. Much better that they believe us, and therefore come to us with their questions, than going to the media or, even worse, their peers, or older kids in their lives.

By age three (or four) we can start introducing the following concepts. It is a good idea to follow their lead when they begin to show interest in where babies comes from and be as truthful and matter-of-fact as possible:

> **What 'sex' is.** For example, a simple explanation of sexual intercourse or 'having sex': 'Penis in vagina to deliver sperm to the ovum'

> **Erections** and what they are for (sex or practicing for sex). ** I have told my 2 year old that his erect penis is 'practicing'. He looks at me, nods, says "Wow", but doesn't know what 'practicing' really means at this age. When he asks for more details I will probably tell him "Your erection is practicing for when you are older. You may want to help make babies by delivering sperm through your penis. To do this it needs to be erect." I will build on the info as he grows and also answer his questions if and when he asks.

How babies are made. Sperm meeting ovum (or 'egg' if we prefer but that can confuse things). There are various ways sperm meets ovum. Again, we can build on this information as they get older/ask more questions.

Lips, mouth and face are private parts. No one likes to be forced to kiss someone else or accept a kiss they don't want. Our mouths are a sensitive part of our bodies and no one should be able to touch them, or our face, if we don't want them to. This concept is well supported in the description and examples given in *Step 2: Teach Boundaries and Consent.*

Simple Examples: We can use examples from the previous age at any time.
"Most girls have a uterus and this is where the baby grows."
"Sperm are the tiny cells that older boys and men make in their testicles. Sperm are needed to make a baby."
"The two tiny cells (sperm and ovum) grow in to a baby inside the mum's uterus."
"The baby doesn't grow in the tummy or stomach because that is where the food goes."
"Sex is something (some) grown-ups do to make a baby." (not the whole storey but a beginning)

"Sex (sometimes) means the man's penis goes inside the woman's vagina to deliver sperm to her ovum."

"Erections are something our penis does to practice what it needs to do to make a baby / when we are older."

"Boys have practice erections so when they get older their penis can deliver sperm to the ovum." "This is how babies are made." (Although this is not the whole picture it is honest and enough for this age).

"A boy has a small hole at the tip of his penis, like yours, where the urine comes out. This hole is called your Urethral Opening. This hole is also where sperm come out when you are older."

"Boys also have another hole in their genital area called the Anus. It is where stool (or poo) comes out." "Girls have one too."

"Labia are some of the folds of skin that are part of your vulva. Yours will grow to look more like Mummy's when you are older. Every woman looks different and that is beautiful."

"Daddy needs to wash your penis well tonight, sweetie. I will gently pull back your foreskin, just a little bit, so I can clean the smegma that is forming there."

Note: I have been told by a pediatric urologist at Children's Hospital in Vancouver that by the time a boy is 3 ½ he should be able to retract his foreskin all the way and clean around the glans and corona of the penis. The corona is the curve at the bottom of the glans (head) of the penis. This is where smegma can build up and infection can potentially happen. It is very important to be gentle when you try to retract and clean your boy's foreskin as other issues may occur. If there is any discomfort, stop. If your boy's foreskin is too tight to be fully retracted by 3 ½, please see a pediatric urologist for advice.

By age three we want to use pictures to help illustrate bodies and babies growing and entering the world. If you are expecting another child your toddler or preschooler will be asking lots of questions anyway! If I had to choose only one illustrated resource to buy for my under 5 year old it would be *It's Not the STORK!*, by Robie H. Harris. It is a good resource to use until age 5, when discussions can get more complex. If you are just starting out with **Bodies, Boundaries & Delight,** and your child is five or older, I would purchase *It's So Amazing!,* instead (by the same author).

Gender Identity Education

In order to start talking about gender it is important to know what it is, and what it is not. Sex and Gender are not the same. Our 'sex' is biologically determined well before birth (including intersexual bodies) and gender is socially constructed. A 'social construction' is something that is created, and constantly re-confirmed, by society. 'Society' includes the people, media and culture we surround ourselves with. Our gender consists of the roles, rules, responsibilities, and expectations we place on each other and ourselves to be, look, and act a certain way. Our sex can be considered as 'what our bodies have' – either on the outside, inside, or what we are expected to have when we are fully developed young adults.

This might come as a surprise, but by age 2 most children have a fairly strong sense of what a 'girl' or a 'boy' is. With this growing awareness our child also can sense where they lay in the socially constructed polarity of male and female. There are some very young children who display strong preferences for gendered toys, colours and activities, and others who are less so, or attracted to what is deemed for the 'other gender'. Some gender preferences have to do with genetics but the majority are due to parental and social influences.

Whether we are the type of person who displays strongly gendered preferences to our growing child, or are more androgynous in our approach, children will learn from us. If we are interested in helping our child to think critically about the world around them we have the choice to broaden their perspective. We can support them to explore 'the other' and open their minds to humanity in general – different cultures, colours and ways of being a family, for example. If any of this appeals, we may be interested in learning about and applying gender identity education (see resources).

We may be motivated to learn and teach about gender identity because we may have a 'tom boy' for a girl or a gentle or 'extra sensitive' boy in our home. It may be quite obvious to us that they don't tend towards typical gendered activities, colours, behaviours, or preferences for activities as the boys or girls around them do. Perhaps we are concerned for them and how they may fair out in the world as they grow and mature. We may want to equip them with tools and knowledge on how to protect themselves from bullying. Perhaps we are afraid they might be homosexual. Whatever your reasons, gender education offers a gift and an insight into 'life'.

We may find it helpful and interesting to grow our awareness of the gendered world we live in, and become more of a critical consumer of it, in order to expand our children's minds. We may learn how we and others play different parts in perpetuating the binaries of female and male and the restrictions placed on children. Restrictions that can cause oppression on behaviours, thoughts, and feelings, which in turn can undermine a budding self-esteem.

Society is changing with regards to gender education and there are more choices now if we choose to play on the 'other side'. Where there used to be little choice when it came to clothes, dolls, games, puzzles, books, etc., now we can purchase and explore a wide variety of 'gender neutral' things. We can follow whatever our child may be attracted to, outside of the norm for their sex.

Some suggestions on how to support our children in their exploration of gender
Try to remain open to what they are attracted to and want to do in their play, instead of guiding them to like what is in the gender norm. Expose them a wide variety of options.

Accept and celebrate that in the first few years of life a child naturally explores whatever is in their environment. For example, a boy may naturally gravitate towards bright colours, like pink, but this doesn't mean he will be gay. A girl may want to play with trucks or toy soldiers because she loves the idea of going fast or being powerful. Try to remain open and encouraging in what they show interest in as this will build their self-esteem and their secure attachment to you.

Children move easily between reality and fantasy. As a parent or caregiver we may bring our reality in to their play too often or too much and miss out on what they are interested in. For example, a boy may want to play Mummy because he wants to explore his nurturing self or be the 'one in charge'. We can support the child's exploration by encouraging them with a smile or nod or by adding other elements in such as buying them their own special doll.

Find, adapt and include simple gender education activities and reflection exercises into our conversations and teaching. Use 'teachable moments' with our children of various ages and show them that what they choose to enjoy or play with may not be what others do but that it is perfectly fine with us!

BBD Step 1: Talking About Bodies

Ages Three to Four

Please review the section above as it pertains to this age as well. Again, it may seem surprising when we view the list of body science words for this age group and see words like sex, sexual intercourse and erections. Remember that society in general, thanks mostly to media, is becoming more open about what sex is and how babies are made. Whether or not we believe this is a good thing, what is important is that we keep up with the education of our children and give them their best start. We may want them to learn what **we** want them to learn (and when) but we also don't want them to be initiated by their peers or the media.

The internet and other media dictates our reality more and more and our children, as young as three and four, are seeing and hearing messages pertaining to sex, bodies and babies on a regular basis. Our children are paying attention and wondering what it all means. They are starting to ask questions. Even if we have a child who doesn't ask questions, they are observers and are **still** curious. All children want to know such basic human things as how are two babies born at once and how were they made? If our child is the type who doesn't 'put themselves out there' it is even more important to have these discussions at this early age and **teach** them to ask questions.

If we make talking about bodies an open subject in our house then even the quiet ones may keep coming to us about private matters as they grow up. Having a trusted adult in a child's life is essential to their well-being and maximum safety. Being prepared ahead of time with the correct information, and how our values play in to the feelings we have and the answers we give, will continue to be an important factor in being that trusted adult, every time.

The following is a list of some of the parts and systems of the body that are involved in reproduction and elimination. These are the most basic body science words to be shared and understood by age four.

Both:	**Nipples, Aereola, Anus, Buttocks, Genitals, Urethra (or Urethral opening), Sex, Sexual Intercourse, Erections, Urine, Stool**
Girls:	**Vulva, Labia, Clitoris, Vagina, Breasts, Uterus, Ovum**
Boys:	**Penis, Foreskin, Scrotum, Testicles, Sperm**

Simple Examples: <u>You can use examples from the previous age at any time.</u>

"Doctors have a word they use for poo, called Stool. In our house we say poo but the doctor will call it Stool." "Poo sure is easier to say, huh?" "We can also say we are going to have a B.M. (Bowel Movement), if we want." "When we poo it is because our bowels <u>move</u> the stool out of our anus. Interesting, huh?"

"Your vulva keeps some of your important body parts safely tucked up inside, like your urethral opening and your vagina. Your vulva and labia will grow and change as you grow and change. Let's look at some pictures of a girl's body and a women's body to see some of the differences I am talking about."

"The opening to your urethra (where urine comes out) is a tiny one just under your clitoris, above your vaginal opening. Your labia and vulva helps cover these openings to the inside of your body as they are delicate and need to be protected from germs."

"The larger, darker ring around our nipple is called our aereola. Can you say that word?"

"Your foreskin helps protect your penis and keep it clean and protected from germs." (If your boy is circumcised you can talk about how underwear helps to protect the penis, etc.)

"Erections are something our body does even when we are growing inside our Mother's uterus. It is a way for the penis to practice what it needs to do when it's older. Erections can happen here and there through the day. Sometimes we wake up with them. They are natural, normal and nothing to be ashamed of."

"Babies are made when a man's sperm meets a women's ovum. This can happen when they have sex." (This is just one way sperm meets ovum but good enough for now! Depending on how your family was created you may want to get the book *What Makes a Baby*, by Cory Silverberg)

"There is a special place in a women's body called the uterus or womb, where babies grow".

(for girls:) "Make a fist and place it right between your belly button and your vulva. This is about where your uterus is and about the size that it is. Cool huh?"

"Babies are made when a sperm meets an ovum. The sperm are (most often) delivered when a man's penis becomes erect and he puts it inside a women's vagina, when she is ready. The woman's vagina will become moist and open a bit so the penis can enter more easily. This is called 'having sex' or 'sexual intercourse'."

"Some people have sex to make babies. Other people have sex because they want to be very close to one another / the one they love and because it feels good." "These things are what grown-ups do, never children".

"You never, ever have to have sex when you grow up so don't worry about that." "It is something people can choose to do when they are older, or not." (I think this is a really important thing to tell little kids because it can seem like a very scary thing to do. They are often relieved to know they <u>never</u> have to do it.)

BBD Step 1: Talking About Bodies

Ages Four to Five

Great Observers, Terrible Interpreters

This year of development brings with it a deepening in what a child notices, attempts to make sense of, and internalizes. They begin to make decisions about more and more complex areas of life. This shift in consciousness can bring with it a host of problems as they are too young to make good sense of what they are taking in. My sister, Kate Saunders, a Child and Family Therapist for over 16 years, explains this well when she tells me that "children are great observers, but pretty terrible interpreters."

We notice more now that our children say things that 'come out of the blue', seem strange or are confusing. The connections they are making in their minds are sometimes bizarre or are full of misinformation or deletions. This is normal and usually nothing to worry about. What their communications offer are chances to correct what they are interpreting and fill in some of the gaps in their observations. These teachable moments are golden and can flow quite naturally as they are curious and easy to teach at this age.

Talk about how many different types of bodies there are – as different as all of our faces – unique and beautiful in their own way. There are great resources out there with excellent illustrations of different bodies that we can show our little ones. I particularly like Robie Harris' book, *It's Perfectly Normal*, which is a great resource to have for our children over 8 or 10 years old. Sometimes it can make us more comfortable if we photocopy the pictures we want to use, from a book for older children, and discuss how and what we feel is appropriate for our 4 to 5 year old around this topic.

The realm of bodies, boundaries and supporting children's curiosity about sensuality and sexuality is a rich teaching area for parents. It is an area of teaching and parenting where the **truth** will help them make good sense of the world around them. Continue to build a straightforward, honest foundation with our children while continuing to remind them about privacy. Many of these topic areas are best talked about at home or in the privacy of a vehicle, for example.

The following is a list of some of the parts and systems of the body that are involved in reproduction and elimination. These are the most basic body science words to be shared and understood by age five. We find more complex ways to talk about each area and add the term 'Sexy':

Both:	**Nipples, Aereola, Anus, Buttocks, Genitals, Urethra (or Urethral opening), Urine, Stool, Sex, Sexual Intercourse, Erections, the term 'Sexy' and what it means**
Girls:	**Vulva, Labia, Clitoris, Vagina, Breasts, Uterus, Ovum**
Boys:	**Penis, Foreskin, Scrotum, Testicles, Sperm**

Talking 'Sexy'

By age five we may want to consider discussing what 'sexy' means and how it is blatantly displayed in our culture. The term 'sexy' has many connotations and its meanings will be important to ensure children begin to understand before they begin Kindergarten. This is nicely supported by the teaching we have been doing up to now about what 'sex' is, how babies are made, and where they 'come from'.

Younger and younger children are acting and dressing like their favorite pop stars and are noticing how the teens and pre-teens dress around them. They may begin to exit the "Princess and Pirates" stage and be turning in to the "Pop Star and Model" stage earlier than we expect. If our four and five year old begins to make this transition at a young age we want to be empowered to help them navigate and understand what they are getting into.

Seeing our children dance and act out what they see in media can be adorable but it can also be disturbing. It is hard not to notice how they move and behave in typically 'sexy' ways. They often like to sing songs with fairly mature lyrics, about sex and relationships for example, as they hear them in movies produced and popularized for their age group. Even if we are very careful with the types of movies they watch, they hear all kinds of songs on the radio or in other forms of media, including very exciting and flashy music videos. By Kindergarten peers begin to have a heavier influence so our children need to be prepared.

Our child may take pleasure in dancing, moving and dressing like their favorite pop or media stars. It is not surprising that children under five have no idea what they are actually seeing in media and what it is communicating. What is surprising is that they already know that what they see is something that is 'cool' or considered attractive. Naturally, our children want this for themselves because they want to be cool and attractive, even if they don't really know what that means. Young children rarely understand what these desires and attractions are and so it will empower them greatly if we, as their trusted adults, teach them in a gentle, loving and supportive way, about what they're seeing, what they're doing, and why.

Talking about what is 'sexy' is a conversation area that belongs in **all 3 Steps:** *Talking about Bodies, Teaching Boundaries and Consent, and Encouraging Curiosity and Delight.* We do our best to begin on a positive note around any and all subject areas that our children take an interest in. "You seem to really enjoy moving your body like that woman on the video. Do you know why she is doing that and what it means to other people?" This is a keystone of media literacy and the more information you can give them the more empowered they will be.

Simple Examples: <u>You can use examples from the previous age at any time.</u>
"Sex is what two people who are attracted to each other do for fun and because it feels good."
"Sex is what two people do to make babies."
"Sex is what grown up people* do with each other because it feels good."
Instead of 'grown up people' you can be more vague (those who like/love each other) or more specific (those who are married) about 'who' has sex and why, depending on your values.
"People dress and dance in certain ways to be attractive to other people. Most music videos are designed this way and you will see

this in all kinds of media. This behavior is all about being 'sexy'. Sexy is also a term like 'attractive' and so others want to be a part of it."

"Being sexy and dressing / moving / acting sexy is a way to communicate to others that you are enjoying your body. It can also communicate that you want to attract someone to be sexy with you or play and enjoy with you."

"Sometimes dancing / dressing / moving in a sexy way is a way to tell someone you want to have sex with them."

For conversations about sex and body science, please see more examples in the age(s) above.

Self-Reflection Exercise

Self-reflection is a crucial part of the journey to being our child's most important sex educator.

Consider these questions and write them in the journal you are keeping:

- How did you learn about your body when growing up? How did you learn about puberty?
- What are your earliest memories?
- From whom or where did you get your information? Was the information correct?
- How do you feel reading the lists of words for each age group? Do you know what each one is referring to?
- How did you learn about sexuality?
- Was there anything you wish your parents had done or said to make you feel more comfortable about your body?
- What might you explain to people who question you on what you are doing and why? For example, "Don't you think they are too young for this information? Aren't the words a bit grown up?" "What's wrong with the word 'vagina'?"

BBD Step 2: Teach Boundaries and Consent

Boundary Intelligence

Boundaries are a fundamental part of our ability to get along with people, protect ourselves, and to acquire what we want in life and in our relationships. We are constantly navigating and negotiating ours and other people's boundaries and requests. This includes getting and giving consent. To 'give consent' is to give permission – a "yes" - to people's requests, whether those requests are verbal/non-verbal, clear/confusing, manipulative or authentically and honestly communicated. Without a doubt, there are countless times we have intentionally or inadvertently crossed someone's boundaries. We make, agree and disagree to requests all day long. Although many of us have not thought about it in this way, we regularly move and communicate within the realm of boundaries and consent.

Children learn very quickly to negotiate with us around our boundaries even **before** they can use words. They are usually trying to tell us something or trying to 'read' us. For example, young babes will use sounds (crying, cooing, babbling), body/head movements, and facial/eye movements to communicate their boundaries and needs to us. A one year old may throw an 'upper level tantrum' that stops immediately if we give in to their request. We can interpret this as an attempt at manipulation or coercion to get what they want – essentially pushing against others boundaries. As children grow they understand more and more what resistances they face and 'how to get their way' in life. They learn how to manipulate, ignore, trespass, fear, yield to, consider, agree with or (eventually) respect others. How human!

As children develop their understanding about what simple boundaries are, and that they too can have them and have people respect them, they grow an essential part of a solid self-esteem and self-confidence. This maturation process can lead to a strong sense of self in most situations which is protective emotionally, mentally, and physically. Having the clarity to know what our boundaries are and be able to communicate them effectively is not only protective but integral to a well-rounded and healthy 'whole self'. It serves us and our children to learn how to have some stronger boundaries and how to honor and respect theirs and others. It is also important to learn to be flexible, to be able to negotiate boundaries respectfully, eventually lose any rigidity that doesn't serve us.

How 'boundary intelligence' translates into sexual health and safety becomes more complex as children mature. Having strong boundaries that can be effectively communicated becomes more and more crucial to protect their well-being on all levels and in most situations.

Emotional Intelligence

Emotional Intelligence (EI) is one of the defining aspects of being able to have and protect personal boundaries. Emotional Intelligence is the ability to understand, manage, and effectively express our feelings. It means we can engage in relationship in a healthy and balanced way and navigate successfully with others' feelings. We can learn to respect both sides of any relationship. The ability to be emotionally intelligent is essential in creating, connecting, developing, maintaining, and enhancing our close relationships.

If emotional intelligence and expressing boundaries in a healthy way is an area of weakness, don't worry. This is an area of the personality and the self that can evolve and increase in strength with our desire to learn and grow. Guided self-reflection via a pathway like coaching is one of the most effective ways to do this. It is often easiest to set our own path of self-discovery and growth by being guided by someone who knows how to 'get there'.

Not surprisingly, the ability to navigate, communicate, feel and express our emotions is a cornerstone to building a secure, empowered, and healthy sexuality. Our children need to be taught emotional intelligence. It is a higher level human trait that often requires guidance of a stronger, wiser, more evolved person to show us the way. And, it takes a lot of safe practice with issues other than sexuality, to bring the skills to navigating healthy and wise sexual boundaries.

Self-Reflection Exercise

If thinking along the lines of boundaries and consent is confusing, consider how you say 'yes' or 'no' to the world around you. Reflect on how you say 'yes' or 'no' to yourself.

Consider how, when and where others cross your boundaries - on a daily basis. How does this feel? What do you do or don't do?

Think about how we constantly teach 'yes' and 'no' to the children in our care. We are teaching them about boundaries and consent all the time. Given this filter, think of some examples that are obvious and that you agree with. Think of some that stretch you or surprise you.

Personal Space and Boundaries

Personal space is one of the first areas in which we teach our children about boundaries. There are some good works out there about 'the personal space bubble' (Hall, 1966) and how to describe who can be inside your bubble, who can't be, and in what context it is safe or appropriate that we extend it out or allow persons in to it. Many children's resources exist to teach this concept like, *No Means No,* by Janeen Sanders. Using the term 'personal space' with our children can begin as young as age one. This education can be made more fun if a game is incorporated into it. There are plenty of great examples online, such as

http://amomwithalessonplan.com/personal-space-activities-for-kids/

Every culture has a different amount of physical space that is considered 'intimate' but the standard is .5 metre (or 1.5 feet). Some cultures are used to having very little space (5 cm or even touching sometimes) and this is still okay between strangers in some situations. Some cultures get uncomfortable when someone comes within 1.5 cm (or 2 feet) of them. Knowledge of intercultural sensitivity about personal space allowances helps us get along better. That said, regardless of what culture we come from we benefit from knowing the fundamental concepts of how to keep our body safe, and when to tell if we have been violated in some way.

This can be better known and understood if we are aware of and teach about 'personal space'.

We may have children who will accept any hug offered and are generally comfortable with touch, and with people being in their personal space. These types of children need more focus on learning to ask before touching. We may have a child who is highly sensitive to touch or doesn't feel comfortable hugging even the closest people in their life sometimes. These types of children need more focus on putting up and protecting their boundaries. We can see these patterns of preference even in our 1 or 2-year-olds.

Depending on our culture and values we can help our children navigate and be sensitive to others' boundaries. One of the ways of doing this is helping them to read people's body language. For example, we may point out people's reactions to loud noises or if someone is throwing garbage on the ground. We can ask our child what they notice about faces and body movements that show fear, anger or other emotional reactions. This type of knowledge and ability to read others' helps our children to respond appropriately to non-verbal communication of preferences or boundaries.

Their Body is Their Own

Respecting our child's comfort levels, regardless of culture, is important to them developing good self-esteem and security. Never force our children to hug, kiss, sit on the laps of, or have any other intimate contact with people they don't want to. This type of forcing crosses boundaries and often equates to a fearful or shameful experience for a child. If our child is a 'hugger' we may find ourselves having to be firm about teaching them other options for hellos and goodbyes. Depending on the circumstances, a wave or a high five can be more appropriate. This type of awareness and education can - literally – mean a change in cultural behavior, and it may be very difficult to do at times, but in this day and age it's crucial. Like training us all to sneeze or cough into our elbow (instead of our hands), the culture of change around touch and personal space is needed. Consent is a much happier, healthier, and safer place to relate from.

You may live in a small town and think boundaries and consent isn't important where we all know each other, but what is protecting our children in this information age, with technology reaching even the furthest corners of our planet? The media our children absorb, inadvertently or deliberately, **every day** communicates many things, including complete rejection of personal boundaries - forcing, coercion, and other violence. Giving them the tools to understand and protect themselves, while understanding and respecting how others feel or behave, is vital to our good citizenship. When living in a mixed cultural environment such as a busy city personal space, boundaries, consent, and knowing what's appropriate public and private behavior can prove to be even more important than in a small town, where the eyes of the community keep a closer watch.

What's Private and What's Public

The basics about what is private and what is public can be taught from year one as toddlers really begin extending themselves into the social world around them. There are private body parts and also private activities. These principles are foundational to the concepts of boundaries and consent. We teach our little ones what is acceptable behaviour in public space and what is meant to be done in private spaces. Public vs. private can be perceived as a large and obvious type of boundary. When our children can understand the differences between public and private we can begin to use the term 'boundary' to start them on the path to understanding this complex part of the social world.

The Mind and Body Connection

"We become what we think about all day long." - Ralph Waldo Emerson

Much research has been coming out of immunopsychological science these days. The mind-body connection can no longer be ignored, denied, or dismissed to the realm of 'new age junk'. What we think affects our body in a myriad of mysterious ways. Who we surround ourselves with, what is said to us, what we internalize or believe to be true, how we experience the world, how our body responds to our environment and what we put in it – all of these every day aspects of life affects our mind and therefore our body.

If what we believe to be true affects our mind, then what we tell our children about their body, and how they experience the world through it, is incredibly important. We build their ability to enjoy life and learn to trust themselves in this world by teaching them to tune in to their senses, their own 'body voice', and to believe what it tells them. No matter what our 'body voice', or intuition, says to us, listening to it and checking in about whatever it is will be protective and productive.

In the words of Gabor Mate, children are motivated by two streams: attachment and authenticity. Authentic communication 'feels' right and good. People who are authentic seem easier to trust because they are honest (at least to themselves!). Children tend to respond positively to authentic people as they are generally safer people. Encouraging our children to experience themselves authentically (honestly) helps to guide their ability to believe others when they are being authentically themselves. This intuition and comfort involves listening deeply to the body and trusting what it says through understanding emotional reactions. If our child is secure with their intuition they can more accurately read safer people and situations. We teach them to listen to their 'gut reaction' which plays a central role in body intelligence. The more they can be accurate in reading situations and people the more protected and empowered they will be.

Peer Pressure Starts Early

Peer pressure begins very early in a child's life. Before our child turns two they usually begin to 'play with' other children, instead of just 'beside'. They begin to watch and be influenced by others as they attempt to engage in shared play. We need to watch our toddlers very carefully at this stage as it is known to be the most violent age. They begin to assert themselves on the world around them, are very self-centered, and are generally incapable of tuning in to how others feel.

One of the first influences, or pressures, seems to be on gender biases. I've watched three year olds attempting to force other children to play with certain toys and not others: "Girls don't play with that! You are silly!" This kind of peer pressure hurts our children, especially if they don't understand what boundaries are and can't protect their thoughts, feelings and curiosities. A child who understands gender and inclusivity, with the language to help them protect their boundaries, can easily respond to such peer pressure: "I can play with whatever I want! I LIKE cars and trucks and that's ok!"

If children bend to peer pressure, or haven't been given the tools and language to protect themselves, they can start to doubt that it is <u>always</u> ok to play with (gender atypical) toys they like. Believe it or not, their sense of self can get bruised and they may start to question themselves unnecessarily. Our sense of self-worth and esteem can be undermined even at this tender age.

Damage to our self-worth can be prevented by a caring adult who believes in and teaches inclusivity. Inclusive education is not just about toys or play preference, but about bodies, family structures, cultures, colours, and more. Peers begin to influence at a far younger age than we hope. We can protect our children, and help them protect themselves, by giving them the permission and the language to do just that.

Media Savvy Parenting

Media Literacy has a complex meaning. This broad area can be described as having critical thinking skills around media message as well as understanding how viewer perceptions actually shape our society and culture as a whole. Media literacy also means a person is able to see and understand what marketers are trying to do or communicate, such as how they manipulate consumers in various ways to change their thinking. Media works to change how we feel about certain aspects of life and to convince us to buy products, or the 'way of life', that is being marketed. For young children media messages become **deeply internalized as reality** - moreso than adults internalize them - until they are taught otherwise. Children are also very susceptible to repetition of media and marketing messages and believe something is 'the best' or 'needed' instead of just wanted.

Being able to describe what media is trying to do to change our thinking will help us to be a media savvy parent. Critical thinking will enable us to make better choices for ourselves as well to teach young ones how also to question the media they consume. Our children can be empowered to investigate any media and ads they see with a critical filter. Pressures to be a certain body type, play with a certain type of toy, dress a certain way - so they don't just 'believe what they see' and feel 'less than' if they don't measure up.

Eventually, as children get older, they begin to recognize how media spins information, how media actually tell lies and attempts to coerce viewers into believing the biases that are put forth. Some common and disturbing messages that get internalized by children are 'boys need to be muscular and big to be good super-hero's' or 'girls need to be pretty and a certain body type' to make friends. Many shows for toddlers, such as Octonauts (almost all male engineer characters and guests), Peppa Pig (mostly follows very traditional gender roles), perpetuate gender biases and oppress without us even giving them a second glance. http://sacraparental.com/2015/07/14/sexism-in-kids-tv-shows-and-movies-what-to-look-for-and-what-to-do-about-it/

As a parent we can help to fight against the oppression by discovering the parts of the storey that are not being told. We can also evaluate media messages based on our own experiences, skills, beliefs, and values, and teach this to our children. Check out **http://medialiteracynow.org/what-is-media-literacy/** Safe internet and media consumption is paramount. We are in charge in these early years and the more we can prepare children, and ourselves, for what happens when they are out of our care, the better.

BBD Step 2: Teach Boundaries and Consent

Ages Birth to One

We are constantly in a dance within the boundary and consent realm. As our consciousness about this important aspect of life and relationship grows we can begin to be more intentional about it. Our wee ones communicate to us in their own special way from birth on. A beautiful thing about this dance is the more we tune in and respond to **their** boundaries and requests the more they trust us. Hence, the better we understand and can appropriately respond to them. Their bond with us grows and attachment and security blooms.

As our awareness and knowledge about ourselves grows via boundaries and consent, the more we may actually *communicate what we want to communicate*. Our authenticity deepens, which makes things easier on parent and child as they can read our signals more clearly. Most importantly, we understand where our boundaries lie and we gain more clarity about how we relate. The more clear we are about how we accept or agree to others requests (or not) the more we will be in alignment with our whole and healthy self. As our whole self comes in to alignment the stronger we will be, the more confident, at peace and happy. All of these amazing qualities, behaviours, and ways of being can be quite effortlessly transferred to our children. Whether conscious of it or not we are a model to them in every capacity, right down to the energetic level.

Simple Examples:
Tune in to your baby as you give baby massage, bath them, or rub lotions or powders on their body. Children give signals of pleasure by cooing, offering smiles, giving eye contact or sighs. They may signal over-stimulation by crunching up their body or face, averting their eyes, or shortening their breath. If they don't like the touch they may cry, wiggle, and clutch their fists. Early communication of boundaries and consent will vary between babies and will grow and change over time. We are already the world's expert with our baby, so enjoy. Acquainting with each other in this first year is an important journey for all.

As they grow, talk with them as you read and respond to their communication:

"Oh, you are enjoying this touch/massage/bath". "It feels good doesn't it?"

"I see you feel overwhelmed. Daddy will stop now."

"Do you need a cuddle? Here, now. Mummy is here for you"

If they turn away you can name the communication: "Have you had enough of Daddy playing with you? I can see you are tired. Let's take a break."

As they approach their 1st birthday and start to cross boundaries, such as reaching for others' toys to chew, or sucking on items that are not clean, we can verbalize the crossing: "Not for eating" "That can make you sick. Here, chew on this" and give them their toy. "That is just for looking and touching". "This is for chewing/eating." When your child tries to chew on Grandma's bracelet (even if her boundaries are ok with it, you may not want your baby exposed to all the perfume, creams, germs, etc.) you can say, "Here baby, let's chew on this instead. That is Grandma's".

BBD Step 2: Teach Boundaries and Consent

Ages One to Two

Practice teaching about Private Parts:

1. Face/Mouth/Lips
2. Breast/Chest area
3. Genital area. This area covers from below the belly button, all the way between their legs, and up to their lower back, including their entire buttock area.

Our toddler is very curious and will often be interested in exploring our private body parts. We may think "how cute" as they stick their fingers and hands in our mouth or nostrils, fondle or squeeze our breasts and nipples, or touch anywhere else we let them. They may also be curious about touching our genitals. It will be important to do some self-reflection on how we feel about our boundaries and being touched or explored in these private areas.

As our toddlers grow we must teach them to ask before embracing a playmate or before touching. Stay positive such as "Let's ask Niko if he'd like a hug good-bye today." If our friend does not want to be touched we can stay positive, smile, and say "That's OK, James. Let's wave bye-bye or blow him a kiss", or, "Sure, no hugs today. Can we give you a high five?" This helps our children to handle the 'no' with grace but also teaches them how to say 'no' when they are feeling that way at another time. Our friend may grow to feel safer around James the next time they meet.

Two Loops of Arousal

Erections can sometimes happen when being touched, especially by gentle hands, and it is important to know a simple fact about our physiology. The arousal network in our body has two loops of feedback – primary (sympathetic), which is the conscious one, and secondary (parasympathetic) which happens without needing any conscious awareness (like our heart beating). When our genitals are stimulated by touch they will usually respond in some form of physical arousal (i.e. erection, lubrication of the vagina, etc.), regardless of how we actually, consciously, **feel** about the touch or the person touching us. For example, when our baby or child touches our nipples or genitals we may experience a sensation of arousal in our genitals and/or an erection. We don't have any sense of sexual arousal in our mind but erections can happen simply from being touched.

When the body responds in this way, at a time when we don't want it to, it can be disturbing, especially if we don't understand that the secondary loop is in action. This feedback loop is doing what the physiology of the body **naturally** does when touched. Female erection doesn't seem to bother many women because no one can see the response that may be happening in our vulva, clitoris or vagina. Yes, our nipples can get erect when we are aroused, but they also respond when we get chilled, are breastfeeding, or feel emotions coursing through us – a common occurrence and usually not an issue for most of us. For many men, however, a penile erection can be uncomfortable when it happens in front of our children, especially when it happens in response from their touching us in their curious moments. Men may react in shame to this experience and feel quite embarrassed.

Once we understand the scientific facts of the secondary/unconscious loop of arousal, it can reduce anxiety in these moments. We may, instead, be able to create a positive, shame-free 'teachable moment' for our children, by sharing information about erections in a simple way (see examples). Don't worry about telling a near two year old 'too much' as whatever they aren't interested in will go over their head. Remember, kids under 5 are very matter-of-fact and naturally have very little, if any, shame about bodies (unless we have inadvertently taught them). Remember, even what we don't say and any non-verbal movements of our body teaches *something* to our child. If we can't find it in ourselves to talk about our erection in the moment, smiling and saying something like "Interesting, huh?" will help keep things light.

Taking advantage of these teachable moments early in our child's life is a way for us to practice being more comfortable talking about the subject **and** for us to be more prepared with accurate, simple answers.

Simple Examples: Feel free to use examples from earlier ages.

As our toddler begins to move and can follow us to places we would prefer them not to be we can gently say to them: "Daddy is going to the bathroom now. I would like some privacy so I will be out in a little while." Or "I love that you are so curious about Mummies body but it makes me a little uncomfortable right now, so I would appreciate some privacy."

If we feel okay about our toddler exploring our body we can say: "Next time we have a bath together, I will let you take a look at my private parts because it is okay that you are curious about my body."

As we experience our toddler exploring the world around them we naturally help them to learn about boundaries and consent: "No, we don't put our hands in people's mouths."

"Mummy doesn't like it when you put your fingers in my nose. Let's go wash your hands."

We teach them how to navigate our bodies and others bodies, such as family, friends and people in different public play situations: "We must take turns with these toys. "It is not okay to hit and grab." "Touch gently."

During bath time or any other situation where Dad is experiencing an erection and is in the presence of his son: "Daddy's penis is becoming bigger, isn't it? When a penis gets bigger and harder it is called an erection. This happens to boys and men and is our body's way of practicing doing what it needs to do to help deliver sperm to make a baby. Even little baby boys, before they are born, will have practice erections. Isn't that cool? You have already had erections. Have you noticed?"

"It goes up and then it goes back down in a few minutes, doesn't it?" "Practice erections."

Or even more simple: "Daddy's penis is becoming hard, isn't it? That is interesting! (smile). Have you noticed your penis getting hard sometimes? It's called an erection." and leave it at that.

If a girl is experiencing this teachable moment, you can say something similar and keep things 'light' by smiling and say "Daddy's penis is becoming bigger isn't it? This is something most boys experience and is a way of practicing for our job of helping to make a baby". This simple explanation is often enough for this age. Remember, though, that giving **more** information than we think they need is always okay, because they will absorb what they are interested in and leave the rest.

Every child is different and some may ask more questions if they are verbal at this age. If we don't feel like getting in to it at the time they ask we can always answer "Good Question" (thanks, Meg Hickling!) and divert the conversation to a later time. Putting off our response offers time to consider how we think and feel about our values and what we want to teach. We can say "Let's talk about this with Mum", or "later, at bath time" or however we want to get some space around the conversation. Be sure to return to it as soon as we can, though, to model that it is important to us to answer their questions.

Before we move on from this tender topic area, remember we always have the choice to prevent our child from every seeing our genitals, or our erection. If this is our preference and some time they do see it and ask, we can put up a boundary in a gentle way, saying something like "These is my private body parts, like your genitals are your private body parts. I feel more comfortable keeping mine private." This is a great way to show them that boundaries are ok and how to communicate them honestly and directly. When we put up a strong boundary it is always softened by a smile, nod, and even some kind of reassuring touch like a hug or a gentle hand on the back.

BBD Step 2: Teach Boundaries and Consent

Ages Two to Three

Good Touch/Bad Touch

Building on what we've been teaching our toddler about boundaries, consent and what is private vs public, is the incorporation of good touch vs. bad touch. As our toddler increases their interaction with the social world, information about private body parts and who is okay to touch them, and when, becomes more important for them to understand and practice. We also teach them what to do if they experience 'bad touch'. Trusting their feelings is important. Teaching them to say NO loudly and move their body away from the situation is important. Teaching them to report any kind of uncomfortable situation or uncomfortable touch to a trusted adult right away is important.

This is a simple yet extremely vital part of teaching our child to protect themselves. There are many great resources to help parents or caregivers about this crucial subject area. I recommend books such as *I Said No! A kid-to-kid guide to keeping private parts private*.

Boundary Intelligence can begin at a very young age. Threats to their body and well-being can come surprisingly early in life and a three year old needs to know exactly what to do to protect themselves. They need the correct terminology for their private body parts, who is safe to touch them and why, and who is not. It is essential to have these life-protecting conversations before any bad touch situations happen. Sexual abuse can happen anytime, anywhere, and research says that most offenders are family members. This type of abuse typically happens with people we know.

Reminder - Private Parts:
- Face/Mouth/Lips
- Breast/Chest area
- Genital area. This area covers from below the belly button, all the way between their legs, and up to their lower back, including their entire buttock area.

We empower our child when we give them information and tools to keep them safe from 'bad touch' situations. The basics of dealing with a potential 'bad touch' situation is, firstly, our child knowing and understanding the following 'safe touch situations':
- who are 'safe' people (usually parents, trusted child care providers, doctors, etc.)
- when is touch safe (bathing, wiping after toileting, diapering, examinations at the doctors when parent is present)

- where is genital touch appropriate (private place like an exam room, bathroom or bedroom)
- how is safe touch experienced (with consent, in appropriate situations, with appropriate people, and done gently)

Secondly, empower our child by teaching them to tune in to their feelings, their body and their intuition. It is a sense that can warn us in situations where 'bad touch', 'bad pictures' or something we feel uncomfortable seeing or doing is happening. These warning signs can be considered a 'red flag' and naming it is as such is an important key to our child being able to protect themselves if these situations arise. Intuition can tell us when 'red flag' situations arise, such as requests made by others to do or say **anything** we feel uncomfortable with, including friends and family. Teach them the basics to protect themselves: to loudly and clearly say NO, to MOVE away, and go immediately to TELL a trusted adult.

Emotional Education and Intuition

Emotional education is something we may already be doing with our children. Being able to share our emotions with each other reduces our child's distress, helps them to communicate more easily and clearly what's going on for them, and supports our ability to help them organize their feelings as they are developing. This type of education builds a good attachment and security for our children. We may be practicing this already, but if not, we can begin to teach our child to name their emotions by labelling our own and helping them to understand and label theirs. This type of emotional education is very helpful for them as their emotions get bigger and more intense. We are all on a wild ride of emotions in our house on a daily basis and, as parents, we work hard to be 'bigger, stronger, wiser, and kind' (Circle of Security).

Intuition is one of our base emotions that the body registers, like fear, love, or frustration and anger. It can be experienced as more complex than fear or love as it includes positive, negative and mixed messages. Between the ages of two and five we can train our child to specifically listen to intuition as part of their body talk and emotional education, easing the topic in to our conversations about 'good touch' and 'bad touch'. Like other complex body sensations, emotions, and relationships, it is best to begin simply and build on knowledge transfer over time.

Your Body is Your Own
Children especially love knowing that their body is their own and they don't have to kiss and hug people they don't want to. This may be challenging for families where culture dictates lots of physical affection, or it may seem bizarre and insulting. Looking from a child's perspective if we give them the power to choose with

whom and when they want to be affectionate, we give them **self-empowerment**, which builds their self-confidence, and self-esteem. Who wouldn't want that for their child? For some this means a total culture shift and can come with some embarrassment and feeling the need to explain. The choice is yours!

When I first began learning about this aspect of boundaries and consent I found it really strange and it proved harder to do than it sounded. Being a natural 'hugger' I had to go against my instincts in order to do this practice. I have had to re-think: do I own these children and can make them do whatever I want them to do, or do I risk my embarrassment and give them more choice and agency as they learn and grow in to the social world? I spent some time unpacking what it means for a child to have this kind of ownership over their body, and their lives, and it was enough to motivate me to make a change. As we incorporated the concepts in our family we eventually became used to 'asking', and guiding our little ones to ask.

Eventually our children began picking up that they had a choice, could tune in to their intuition and choose what they wanted to do in the moment. They are becoming more comfortable with doing what **they** want to do to greet, thank, or say goodbye in their own way. They sometimes remember to ask others if they want to be touched! This gives me great comfort as we are confident they will be able to keep up their body ownership and read boundaries in situations when we are not there.

We are trying to change our ingrained behavior patterns and so we can't keep on top of this practice all the time, in every location. People aren't really trained on this concept yet and things happen quickly in most social situations. Not too many of us are aware of this type of consent with children and aren't practicing it yet, but it is coming. This type of generalized social change takes time and education, like the sneezing into the sleeve thing...

Especially by the age of three a child needs to understand that their body is their own. One of the ways we can encourage this body pride is to have them wash their own genitals during bath time. Depending on our situation we will be continuing to help them from this age, up, but having our child understand that their genitals are important, and that they need to take good care of them, helps to teach them a sense of ownership over their body.

Self-Reflection Exercise

Think back to times when you were a child and your parents pushed you to receive or give affection. Maybe it was a Grandpa who always wanted a kiss on the mouth? An Auntie who hugged you too hard, pinched you somewhere or generally made you feel uncomfortable? Recall, perhaps, your family forcing you to kiss, hug, or sit on the lap of friends, family members and sometimes literal strangers (to you). How did that make you feel? Did you wish you had a choice, and your parents' support, to help you greet or thank someone in your own way?

Culturally we have more choices now with waves, smiles, handshakes, high fives, and other forms of greeting that don't involve our boundaries being crossed, or our private parts (i.e. mouth, chest or buttocks) getting involved.

Think back also to times when our older peers, siblings or cousins coerced us into seeing or doing something we didn't want to. There are probably some examples of when this happened to you, or you tried to convince others to do or look at things they didn't want to. How do you feel this affected you and your experience of life growing up? How may it be affecting you now?

Proofing Strategies for your Preschooler

ɔught! Porn proofing my three year old? Even children as young ɔ three can be exposed to 'bad pictures' as pornography and pornographic type images are insidiously planted all over the internet. Some advertisements and TV shows can also border on the pornographic, or at least too much for our children under 5 to see. Having some kind of conversation about 'bad pictures' (pornography, violence, or other scary/inappropriate media) with your 3 to 4 year old will be an important protection mechanism, especially before they go on a play date where there may be older children or teens present.

Although 3 and 4 year old children may not be ready for a book such as *Good Pictures Bad Pictures*, it will be protective to give them a simple explanation and specific plan to keep themselves safe if they ever get exposed to porn or other violence on TV or media.

For Porn-proofing, try a scenario like this:
"Remember when Daddy / Mummy talked about what sex is? Well, sometimes people take videos and pictures of people having sex and put these videos on the Internet. This is called pornography. Porn is something I want to you avoid completely and something we can talk a lot more about when you're older. In the meantime,

if you **ever** see these kinds of pictures or videos let's have a plan for you to protect yourself!"

First: Close your eyes and turn away from anything that looks like people having sex. Shut the computer or device.

Next: Call out what it is - say "This is porn!" (get them to practice that with you in a loud voice).

Then: Get away and go tell a trusted adult as soon as possible that you have been exposed to pornography.

Adapted from *Good Pictures/Bad Pictures*

Ensure that everyone in the family is on the same page. If someone in our house uses porn be extra careful to safe guard other users on any shared devices that our child may get their hands on.

Simple Examples: You can use examples from the previous age at any time.

"You don't want to give your grandpa a hug or kiss hello, today? That's okay! How about a hi-five or a handshake?"

"Let's say thank you for the visit/present! How would you like to do that? Hugs or kisses are nice or you can shake their hands and say thank you! What do you feel like doing today?"

"You can choose how you want to say goodbye because your body is your own, right?"

"I know you love to give hugs, sweetie, but some people don't feel comfortable all the time. Can you see how that person is moving away when you open your arms? Let's try giving them side hug, or maybe a handshake, or wave."

"Not everyone likes kisses and that's okay." You love kisses, don't you? You can give Daddy a kiss but let's find another way to say hello to our friends, okay?"

"We must always be gentle when we touch our friends and sometimes they don't like it even if we are gentle. Always ask before touching." "Everyone's body is their own, right?"

"Daddy needs to wash your genitals. I am gentle when I wash your vulva and anus but it's important to keep them clean, right?"

When someone has been rough with them: "It hurts when someone is rough with you, isn't it? This is a kind of 'bad touch'. Being touched gently and kindly feels good, though, doesn't it? Only when we want to be touched, though, right? Your body is yours."

"I could see that you didn't like it when Uncle wanted to pick you up and didn't ask. It's ok to say no to touch and offer a wave instead."

"Sometimes our intuition, or our body, can tell us a situation or a hug doesn't feel good so it's important to listen to that and get away or say no."

"Are you feeling scared? Sometimes a thing called our intuition is trying to tell us something. Did that person make you feel uncomfortable? It is very important to listen to our intuition."

"It's sometimes okay to look at each other's private parts/play these types of games but only if it is okay with **everyone**. Always stop whenever someone says to or moves away, okay?"

Siblings

"I can see that you and your brother are exploring each other genitals. It is interesting to look at another person's private body parts?" "Let's be sure everyone is ok with this, right?" (Smile - be encouraging/not shaming). At this age I would stay around to make sure what's happening is consensual and brief. They will probably stop and may feel awkward but we are there to protect the younger one, especially.

"Your brother is saying no to what you are doing. Please listen and respect his boundaries."

"You are hurting your sister when you're sitting on her. She is crying! Please listen to her feelings and get off her."

"When your sister kicked you in the vulva it really hurt, right? We must be gentle with our genitals and protect them at all times."

"It is not okay to touch our brothers' penis/scrotum/ testicles/ anus without him saying yes. If he says it's okay, but then he turns away or says no, you must listen and stop."

"Our genitals hold the parts that helps us to make babies so let's keep extra care of them in case we want to have one, one day."

"It is never ok to touch our sister's private parts without asking. This includes her mouth/lips, breast area or genital area. If she says it's okay but changes her mind you must immediately listen and stop."

"The person who says No, Rules." (Thanks, Meg Hicking!)

BBD Step 2: Teach Boundaries and Consent

Ages Three to Four

Children this age are often in group care situations, out on playdates, and sometimes go to sleepovers with family or peers. Some have siblings and much of their play can be unsupervised. Children of this age often take opportunities to explore others, or are exposed to others wanting to explore them. It is vital to arm them with the words and actions to protect themselves (see the resource *"I Said No"* – Trust their Feelings, say NO loudly, move away from the situation, report to trusted adult ASAP).

As discussed, is imperative for our children to understand and respect other's 'no's. It is **essential** for our children to know what boundaries they must keep for themselves, **especially** if they are the curious ones. Review the resources listed for good touch/bad touch and continue to teach them about safe people, safe touch, and good boundaries and consent practices.

Our child may become more interested in wanting to explore theirs and others' bodies more often. They may begin self-pleasuring type practices, and explore using objects or doing inappropriate things to themselves or others at times. They also may start asking questions about the good feelings they have when they touch themselves or rub against things with their genital area. Already having the words about body parts and behaviors that are healthy and appropriate are important at this time, so it is great that we have been practicing. We can see how we can build on what they already know - and what we are comfortable talking about - as we teach about this more challenging subject area. There is more information about healthy self-pleasuring and exploration in **Step 3: Encouraging Curiosity and Delight**, but I will go over a few important boundary and consent points here.

When we have already taught our children about public and private areas and activities we can more easily remind them about boundaries around self-touch. If this is within our value system we can let them know that self-pleasuring is a healthy activity, that is okay to do, but must be done in private, which means alone and in their bedroom. We can remind them that their body is their own and another person's body is also **their** own. Depending on the focus of our child, and the activity we see them engage in, we can remind them that other people's bodies do not belong to the curious one. **Whoever says or feels 'No', rules, and this must be respected**. Helping them to tune in to body language of the friends or siblings they are beginning to explore with will be important and protective.

Reading Body Language

Body language has its own complex cultural, familial, and societal rules and meanings. Depending on where we come from we can teach our children by pointing out different things that people do when they are uncomfortable or are trying to say 'no' in their own way. In many cultures people tend to turn their bodies or faces away from a situation that they don't want to engage with. Our children can tune in to how they do this themselves when they feel a 'no' inside.

We can support our children to understand that a 'no' can be hard to read sometimes. Sometimes people don't have the words to say no, or they aren't sure how they feel and need time and space to figure it out. We can point out examples, for instance, when a person just looks down or away but doesn't say anything, even when asked. Teaching our children to acknowledge and accept these subtle ways of saying 'no' will be important as they grow and are able to read body language. We basically show our children examples as they happen - where body language is communicating that a person is not comfortable and that the child needs to stop and move away. Sometimes a person will put their hands behind their back, squirm on the spot, put their head down or away, saying nothing or "ummm". We teach that these are all examples of less direct ways of saying 'no' and should be respected.

On the other end, when we have consent we have agreement. Most agreements should be clear, enthusiastic and easy to read like a "Yes, I'd like to." or "Yes, for sure!" or "Sounds like a great idea. Let's do that!" Some agreements or consent can be non-verbal, including big smiles, nods, moving our body towards, opening our arms for hugs, pursing our lips and moving our head forward, holding our hand up for a shake or fist bump. When it comes to sexuality, or sexual touch in any form, one should be getting an enthusiastic and clear 'yes' that continues throughout the experience. Nothing else is true consent.

Body Exploration

When we find our child exploring their genitals, try not to bring our embarrassment or shock to the situation. Gently remind them to do this in private if we find them in other parts of the house. This type of exploration is a natural thing for them to do and we can be very supportive if we just accept it and remind them to wash their hands after and give them their privacy.

If they come up with a question when we find them exploring themselves, and we don't feel equipped to answer in that moment, we can choose to say "Good Question"! "Let's talk about that when you are done and have washed your hands." Or if we are comfortable we can answer their questions there and then, pointing out their body parts, giving them their scientific names and functions.

Smegma – a special mention!

When I've seen my girls explore their vulva they have asked questions about 'the white stuff' in the folds of their labia or under their clitoral foreskin. The scientific word for this substance is smegma and it may be present depending on when they last bathed, how thoroughly they washed their genitals, or if they have a yeast infection. A simple answer is that it is a natural substance the body produces to keep these body parts clean and lubricated, and that it washes away in the bath quite easily (on girls).

Penis' are a different storey (surprised?): Foreskin is a very special organ and part of what it does is produce smegma - for lubrication, protection and natural cleaning of the glans (head). A baby boy's foreskin should be gently washed – outside and in - but not be **fully** retracted until the age of about 3 ½ or 4. The process of retracting a toddler's foreskin can be done slowly as they grow and age, with the goal that it can be stretched over the glans (head) of the penis so that under the corona can be cleaned also. This process is done so that smemga can be cleaned out from under the foreskin. By the time he is 3 ½ or 4 years old our aim is that there is no build-up of smegma, which has the potential to cause infection.

We can start this careful cleaning process when our baby boy is about 18 months but please be very gentle when retracting the foreskin and revealing the tip of the penis and urethral opening. There is a potential for damage if the foreskin is pulled back with any pressure whatsoever at this age, so best done at bath time, tuning in to and communicating with your toddler if any touch feels uncomfortable. They are usually interested in what you are doing as there are a lot of sensations and a better view of his urethral opening - a rich ground for *Step 1: Talking about Bodies*. Ask for guidance from a specialist if you have any questions. (If you have chosen to circumcise your baby boy then you chose to surgically remove his foreskin and this doesn't apply to your situation.)

Body Exploration - -Siblings/Cousins/Peers

When we find our child, under four, exploring other bodies there is a few important things to consider and communicate, for the situation to be safer:

Are they the same age or within a maximum of 1 year of each other?

Are they the same gender?

What is the power difference between them (more confidence, more vocal, older sibling, male vs. female?)

Do they seem comfortable and enjoying themselves (i.e. smiling, giggling)?

Are they doing it in private?

I would ask if everyone is okay with what is going on, read their faces and the situation and if all seems well, quietly close the door and leave them to it. (!!) This tender place of boundaries and consent can be a difficult one to navigate. If we get a sense that whatever is happening is inappropriate and not okay with one of the kids (we can ask), have them take some time to wash their hands and redirect them to another activity. All the while try to keep calm and neutral.

Creating a teachable moment out of this situation would be a good idea. Depending on what was happening and how we read the comfort levels, it might be a more urgent situation to talk about in the moment or, perhaps, something gentle to bring up near bedtime. Either way, have a conversation about boundaries and consent, using the example as a teachable moment. If applicable, it would be a good idea to tell the other child's parent, but not in front of the children, so as not to shame or embarrass them. Children are innocently navigating the world of bodies at this point and keeping their self-esteem intact is a big step towards them having a healthy self-worth later in life. They will also tend towards hiding things from us if we shame them.

In our family, sometimes our children's play includes some boundary crossing and I always stick up for the one who is saying 'no'. We are also **very clear** that our youngest, only 2, can't 'consent' to any type of genital touch or exploration from his sisters so they must only do that when a parent is around. Of course, our son needs to have an enthusiastic 'yes' to any requests to be touched, and we keep it brief and light. We also take the time to remind him to <u>always</u> tell Mum or Dad if anything happens to him that he doesn't like.

If a sibling group included an older boy and younger girl I would be much more diligent about any kind of sensual play between them. I would recommend explaining that the boy typically has more power in these types of situations because he has a penis. When erect, a penis can hurt another person if used without consent. I would remind them that whoever says 'no' always rules and generally keep a close eye as they get older.

Why do I bring this up between the ages of three and four? Because I have countless stories from my parent education workshops where a parent opens up to the group about their sexual abuse or harassment that they sustained from their older siblings and cousins. Generally this happened when they were four or older. It is always a tragic tale for me to hear and something that I believe could have been avoided with education. Imagine if we were equipped with body science and language, and the rules of boundaries and consent, how different our lives might have been? We must give our children these tools and knowledge, before they might ever need them. As they are old enough to understand, it is essential for them to internalize that even though things feel good doesn't mean we do them whenever we want and to whomever we want.

If this kind of thing has happened to you I encourage you, with all my heart, to find support to release these traumas and be on a path of healing. Explore a professional who is skilled at holding space and helping survivors to heal and move on. I wish the deepest courage and clarity for you if this is something you choose to do.

Simple Examples: Please review the examples from the previous age and feel free to use them.

"I see that you are exploring your genitals. I am glad that you are doing this in private, sorry to interrupt you. Please wash your hands after and before you do anything else."

"Do you have any questions about your body parts?"

If you find your children in some form of nakedness and exploration of private parts: "It looks like you are exploring each other's bodies? Is your friend okay with this game? Maybe our friend doesn't know but remember, this behavior is very private and some people can feel very uncomfortable so please make sure you ask before every kind of touch. Make sure the person says yes and really means it."

"You can stop any time. Just move away and if you feel uncomfortable please tell an adult."

"Honey, I know you are very curious about bodies but remember their body belongs to them, just like your body belongs to you, and they may not feel comfortable even if they seem like they are."

When talking about sexual intercourse from a women's perspective: "When a women's body is ready, sex can feel very good. If the woman is not wanting to have sex her vagina will not open or moisten and sex can be very painful." "If someone forces someone else to have sex this is called 'rape' or 'sexual assault' and is very serious and illegal".

"Whoever says 'No' rules" (Meg Hickling, Speaking of Sex, 1996). Teach your children this over and over!

BBD Step 2: Teach Boundaries and Consent

Ages Four to Five

For this age group, I encourage you to build on what has already been being covered and reinforced through time and experiences over the first four years. Feel free to bounce around the Steps and use the examples and topics of other age groups as situations arise. The year between four and five is a big growing year and their brains are starting to develop much more complex pathways of thinking and experiencing the world, relationships and media. More than ever our five year olds become more interested in, and influenced by, the media and their peers. We can be prepared by deepening the teaching we have been building on.

The Term 'Sexy'

The term 'sexy' will be important to ensure they understand by age 5. Based on knowing what 'sex is', through our earlier conversations about body science, our child may take pleasure in dancing, moving and dressing in ways that we consider 'sexy' in our culture. They may also like to sing songs not typical for a four to five year old – hmmm. You may also not see **your** child perform in this way but want to be prepared as their friends are doing it!

Being prepared is a good thing, even if your children don't seem to be into this type of thing. We inevitably hear all kinds of songs on the radio or in other forms of media, including music videos. It is not surprising that children under five have no idea what they are actually seeing or doing when consuming this type of media. What they do know is that it is something that grown-ups do that is 'cool', and typically something they consider to be very attractive. Children want this for themselves because they want to be 'cool and attractive', even if they don't really know what that means. At this point, young children rarely understand what these desires and attractions are but are an ideal age to learn a bit about it. It will empower them greatly if we teach them in a gentle, loving and supportive way about what they're seeing, what they're doing, and why.

Talking about what is 'sexy' is a conversation area that belongs in all *3 Steps: Talking about Bodies, Teaching Boundaries and Consent, and Encouraging Curiosity and Delight*. Believing it is always best to start on a positive note around any and all subject areas that our children take an interest in, we can talk about being 'sexy' like this: "You seem to really enjoy moving your body like that woman in the movie. Do you know why she is doing that and what it means to other people?" This area of sex education falls under media literacy as well. The more information we can give them the more empowered they will be.

Pornography and Porn-Proofing your Child

It is important to prepare our children **before** they need the tools and information. This can come much younger than we would expect or hope, due mostly to technological advances. To illustrate, I share a storey of parents who were taken aback when they found their 6 year old, and friend, watching pornography on their smartphone during a play date. Back storey goes that these close friends were already exploring their bodies by peeing on each other during shared bath times - nothing unusual there, if we think about it. Tides changed when they innocently took this exploration further into the world of media. They got a hold of a parents' smartphone and voice-spoke a search into Google - "boys and girls peeing". I am sure it comes as no surprise that hard core pornography came up on the screen. These kids just stared – taking in all those 'bad pictures' - until a parent heard the sounds and came running. Shock on all counts … some questions, and a fast lesson on *'Good Pictures/Bad Pictures'* was needed (a little too late).

It's just that easy. I know of many young children, ages ranging from 9-12, who have become porn addicts due to unsupervised screen use by unsuspecting parents. These children's sexuality have been and will be negatively affected by this early exposure. Even if young people feel that early exposure hasn't bothered them, and has not affected their brain or sexuality, the research states otherwise. http://yourbrainonporn.com/adolescent-brain-meets-highspeed-internet-porn Unfortunately, both boys and girls begin to believe that what they see in these images is are normal bodies or healthy sexual behaviour. Boys and girls suffer this twist on reality and, although 5 years old seems young, we must keep up with this technological age.

Societal ethics can't keep up with the technological advances so we must do what we can to protect our children. The best defense is talking about it - educating our children by giving them critical thinking skills and a plan to save themselves from the ravages of these 'Bad Pictures'.

There are not many books available today to help parents talk to and teach their children about the dangers of pornography on the brain and on their self-esteem and healthy sexuality. Good Pictures Bad Pictures –would be important for us to read before our child is 3 or before any playdates where there are older siblings around. The book is certainly fine to read to our 5 year old but best done in chunks as the content is heavy and invites lots of discussion. Most importantly, all parent and professionals working with children could read this book and be prepared in advance. There is power in teaching our children these important topics as soon as we feel they can understand. Media is all around us and we need to prepare as best we can, educate, and work those 'teachable moments'.

Self-Pleasuring and Boundaries

We will be talking a lot more about this subject in *Step 3 Encouraging Curiosity and Delight*, but **safer exploration** of bodies is done within the realm of boundaries and consent. Babies and toddlers will naturally discover and want to explore and play with their genitals. Some start before their first year while others don't take much interest until their second year, or after. Usually boys begin this activity earlier than girls and we can probably understand why – their penis, scrotum and testicles are much more easily accessible. Touching one's genitals for children under five is generally done for comfort and through the lens of curiosity. It is nothing to worry about as long as they have clean hands, are being gentle with themselves, and are working towards always doing this in private.

As children learn that touching their genitals feels good, they may want to do it more and more. It is a healthy and normal practice but of course, everyone feels differently about this and when and where it is ok to do it. We can decide for our children what is appropriate, and when and where - if we allow it at all. An important thing is that they learn to touch/comfort/pleasure themselves in private.

When I researched for resources on self-pleasuring and boundaries for children, I found very little. None of what I found was really appropriate for children under 5. This is not surprising considering the amount of taboo there is about the subject in just about **every** society on the planet. In Robie H. Harris' book, *It's Perfectly Normal*, (pg.48), there is a gentle and simple explanation with images that are mild. Although this book is for 10 and up, I think by age 7 most children will benefit – times are changing and school, and the world, are not what they used to be!

The Ravages of the Social World

As my eldest daughter entered kindergarten I was aware that she never seemed to care much what she wore or how she acted. Within a few months of being in elementary school, at the tender age of 5, she claimed she wanted to be the most popular girl in class and could I tell her how to do this? (!) I was confused and a little scared as to what this focus actually meant for her and she wasn't able to explain her distress. As we may know, and will definitely find out, our children say very little about what happens at school and when pressed often answer in short, uninformative statements. My daughter hadn't been concerned with this kind of thing until that time, so what happened? It wasn't until a year later that I finally began to understand that she was having trouble connecting with kids and was being excluded by the cliques already forming (in kindergarten!). What she made this mean was that no one liked her and that she was powerless to do anything about it.

I thought I had equipped her with the tools and attitude she needed to do well in groups such as school or daycare. I trained her to watch interactions between kids and notice what is happening. Along the lines of teaching her about using her intuition, I worked to get her used to observing behavior and checking in on what she saw. What I didn't think about with my first was that in large group school situations things are a different storey all together. The child to adult ratio is much less and a great deal of misbehaving goes on without adult supervision. That and the fact that children can be cruel even if they are raised to be 'good kids'.

We do our best to prepare our children for what I call the ravages of the social world. "Your peers at school are saying mean things to you? Some people are mean to others to make themselves feel better or to seem 'cool' or tougher. If you feel you can do it, tell them it is not ok to talk like that. Tell a trusted adult at school what is happening, avoid the offending peers when you can, and remember you can decide for yourself what you believe." To help boost their self-esteem I remind them of their worth by pointing out the many aspects of themselves that are special.

Being our child's best and closest advocate is highly protective. So is inviting as many of the children in their class over to your house for playdates as possible. I did this in order to get to know the children better, and as much as I could, their parents. As we are beginning to understand, boundaries and consent become increasingly important to teach children at this age. The social world becomes more of an influence as our children have more autonomy and are away from their loving parents and caregivers more and more.

When my daughter started having more low-supervised playdates, my eyes were really opened to the different levels of social and emotional education children had received. I overheard things that raised the hairs on the back of my neck or threw into question what kind of upbringing these children had received! I also came to learn how some children weren't 'safe people' to be around my child. I believe it is important in these early social days that we be as involved and/or informed as possible for several reasons. For example, to get a sense of how our child interacts in the 'real world' - what amount of power they give over or try to have over others -

and to guide and educate them on how to maneuver and protect themselves in various situations.

When thinking about the ravages of the social world, giving our preschoolers and kindergartners the best start possible begins with the type of education that I describe in this book. Once they are in the hands of their peers and are exposed to the kinds of media influences that we don't necessarily agree with, things will start to change. Our children can be protected with our open sharing of topics such as bodies, boundaries, and sexuality education. Following what is age-appropriate, the more they know the better, and before they need to know it.

Some Examples: <u>We can use examples from the previous age at any time</u>. Please also see the examples incorporated throughout each sub section. As we know, the concepts in Ages Four to Five are more complex so the examples are not as simple!

When you see your child using sexy type dance moves and singing lyrics that might seem too old for their age you can use this as a teachable moment. "That singer is dancing in a sexy way. Do you see how she is moving her body? I can see how you are doing that too. Does it feel good?"

"People like to dance like this because it feels good. Sometimes they are moving this way because they are trying to be sexy or attractive to other people. Remember when we talked about sex and what that means? It is important to know because we want to be clear about what we communicate to people by how we move."
"Dancing in a sexy way is also fun and should be a fine thing to do whenever we want but sometimes it's best to do sexy things in private or around trusted adults." "It's good to be aware."
"You see how that show/commercial/ad talks about how we have to be a certain way to be cool?" "This type of communication can make people feel like they aren't good enough as they are and need to change. This is not a healthy message and it's not true. What do you think?"

With Siblings/Cousins/Peers

"It is okay to want to look at others bodies but we must always ask if it is ok with them and **always** stop when they say no or move away."

Direct all siblings and cousins, especially younger ones, how to say NO and actively get away from their older siblings - and to go tell a trusted adult what happened, right away.

BBD Step 3: Encourage Curiosity and Delight

Supporting Your Self-Discovery First

The concepts involved with *Encouraging Curiosity and Delight* is at once progressive and yet is a natural event of parenting. In the realm of sex education Step 3 can be utilized simply as a way for us to engage in self-reflection about where we stand and how we feel about children's *natural curiosities* and explorations. In this task, it may be helpful to explore the culture around us, our family group, or the larger society.

Our self-reflection may prove very insightful, and perhaps even painful, as we recognize and perhaps re-live the oppression and shame that we faced growing up. For example, the memory of 'being caught' and humiliated or judged may still be limiting us today. We may be continuing to experience the oppression of this type of early shaming in our adult sexuality, today. I have helped many clients to release this kind of trauma on their path to sexual empowerment.

A big part of *Step 3 - Encouraging Curiosity and Delight* is **self-reflection**. How do we feel about the potential of repairing the shame and guilt we may have within ourselves? How can we empower ourselves to express our own sexuality in a healthy way?

When we explore ideas of how to help our child be more fully expressed than we were growing up, how do we feel and why?

The word *Delight* seems to make a lot of sense when we think about very little children. It is an emotion and expression that comes easily and often as our little ones grow, learn and develop. We often say that 'delighting in children' is one of the greatest benefits there is to being in the challenging and rewarding role of caring for them. Caring for children can also be overwhelming and scary, monotonous and boring, and without a doubt, emotionally and physically draining. Spending more time delighting in them helps to balance the load.

Delighting in our children's exploration of their sensuality and sexuality can be a natural part of our parenting process and experience, albeit a daunting one. Some parents never want to consider the pathway our children take to discovering and enjoying the pleasures of their body (and eventually others' bodies). For many it is unheard of to even think or worry about this kind of stuff - until they are teens, right? If we choose to support our child's self-discovery and enjoyment of their sensuality and sexuality, this task can be made easier if we reflect on and understand how natural this exploration is – how human. Thinking back to our own path can provide clarity and guidance for how we want to be with our children.

Fear of societal and familial judgement often stands in the way of delighting in our own sensuality and sexuality, and being on a path of encouraging our children to delight in theirs. Often we can be hindered by the deep-rooted shame and fear we feel about sexuality, which is typically based on our early life experiences and how we were raised. When we see our children exploring sensually or sexually, our memories may come flooding back. Some memories can negatively affect how we behave toward our children in the present. Memories about how we were shamed and shut down when we explored and delighted in our bodies (and eventually others' bodies), can haunt us today. We can, inadvertently, pass on these negative, shameful messages to our children.

Step 3 – Encouraging Curiosity and Delight is one in which we explore deeply the meanings that we make about our sensuality and sexuality, how it grew and developed within us, and what we would like to pass on or not pass on to the children in our life. For some of us this whole concept and notion is just too challenging to consider. If you are one of those people, I encourage you to take time to read through and reflect before making a decision to skip

Step 3 altogether with your children or simply to close this book. Bear in mind that the information within this Step has the potential to increase your happiness and, well, what have you got to lose?

Sex Positive Parenting – not for everyone

Although *Step 3 – Encourage Curiosity and Delight* may prove challenging or impossible for some parents and caregivers, for others it may come as a welcome relief. Some parents and caregivers may be looking for guidance on how to undo society's chains to enjoying our sensuality and sexuality. Some may want to foster a healthy attitude and experience for the children in our care. Some parents may consider themselves a 'sex positive person' and have no idea when or how to transfer our values on to our children.

A research-based description of 'Sex Positive' is defined by Carol Queen as "…the cultural philosophy that understands sexuality as a '*potentially*' positive force in one's life, and it can, of course, be contrasted with sex-negativity, which sees sex as problematic, disruptive, dangerous."

> *Queen, Carol; Comella, Lynn (2008). "The Necessary Revolution: Sex-Positive Feminism in the Post-Barnard Era". The Communication Review.* **11***(3): 274–291.* *doi:10.1080/10714420802306783.*

'Sex positivity' has many meanings and connotations but in the realm of this book it is brought back to its most basic form. Parents supporting their children - birth to five – to enjoy the pleasure of their senses, their natural curiosity about bodies, and to encourage them to delight in themselves as they develop their self-awareness and self-esteem. Extending out into the social world as they begin having playdates, sleep overs, or be involved in large group care, our children are taught to engage with others in a safer and consensual way.

Children raised with 'sex positive' education will have added safety and security to report anything uncomfortable or unhealthy, as they have a strong bonds with Trusted Adults. As they grow into pre-pubescent 6-8 year olds they will see nothing wrong with enjoying their body and learning about how it will change. They will eventually understand and celebrate as they discover the pleasures of their body in puberty, and how much stronger these sensations and urges become. Feeling confident and having strong boundaries about what is safe, healthy and appropriate, they will enter the years where they may explore others (with even less supervision). With tools and knowledge in place they will be able to navigate these precarious and potentially dangerous waters effectively - keeping themselves (and others!) safer and happier.

My goal for young people (and adults) is to be truly empowered in their whole self and in their sexuality. My intention for teens is that through this lifelong empowerment path they are balanced on the path of sexual self-discovery. They aren't consumed by or obsessed with sexuality and are kept safer during this potentially dangerous time. If we raise our children to be 'sex positive' then sexuality and its healthy expression is something that has always been there as a natural and normal part of life. My intention is that teens are safer from the ravages of porn

(http://yourbrainonporn.com/adolescents-pornography), safer from the detriment the media has on their blooming self-esteem and sexuality, and probably most important, safer from their peers.

To be a 'sex positive parent' means we will support our child's sexual and gender identity however it emerges. Sex positive parenting is an attitude and a belief that assumes our children will develop into autonomous, sexually active adults. We support them as they grow into their unique sexual and gendered selves' - which means we have constant open conversations and teaching moments from the very start.

Consent is the basis of all healthy sexual activity and I expand on this keystone belief in *Step 2: Teach Boundaries and Consent*, for every age and stage. We are the expert of our children so find what works for us, what works for them, and then work to close the gap. We _can_ do this challenging work and we don't have to do it alone. Spend time with the references and have courage to find the support you may need.

Self-Reflection Exercise

Take some time to identify the gap between what you **want** to teach your child and what you actually feel **capable of**. Reflect on your wish list for your child and their self-esteem/self-worth/sexual self-esteem.

If we are just beginning the path of parenthood we are fortunate in that this journey will be an easier and more gentle one. For parents with children under 2, we have time to get informed, get comfortable, and ready ourselves for what is to come. If we are parent to children already 4 or 5, things may be a little more challenging for us at first but we can get caught up in time for them starting Kindergarten.

It may take more effort and planning if we are just beginning this journey to becoming our school aged child's Trusted Adult but there are plenty of good resources for parents of this age group. One that I recommend, and has been published in 2017 by a very reliable set of sex educators, is Saleema Noon and Meg Hicklings's book *"Talk Sex Today"*. If I was to purchase **one book for parents or professionals**, to reach a pre-pubescent child (6-8), one already in puberty (8+), and older teens, it would be this one.

Remember that they need this information well '**before**', so, start anywhere and as soon as possible if your child is over 8. If our preference is to give them a book and then answer any questions (The Big Talk), then I would use an age appropriate children's resource like *"It's Perfectly Normal"*. Whichever children or teen book you purchase I recommend reading the book first, and then give it to your child or teen. Let them know that once they are done you will sit with them and answer any questions they may have (if this is something you can or want to do). Take into account that what you are modeling to them already speaks volumes. It would be valuable to dig deep and make some clear decisions about what you are going to do and say ASAP. Getting more support for this may be important for you. Coaching is a great pathway to guidance and change.

As you identify and work to close the gaps between what you **want to be like** and what you are **actually being like**, you are becoming more of your whole self while showing your children how to be their whole self. Modelling is a potent messenger. As I shared earlier, this is constant work in progress for our family too! Perfection is impossible and unwanted – we go for 30%!

Exploring the World through our Senses

Let us reframe how we experienced the world of sensuality and sexuality and give it fresh eyes. We begin with exploring our senses. In the earliest days of our lives almost all our affection, love and security was communicated through touch, sounds, smell and tastes. The same goes for our baby. Over the first 4 or 5 years of their lives, we can encourage our child to explore the world in a deeper way through their senses. We can guide them to be aware of and to enjoy the process of finding pleasure (or other) in the world around them more and more. We also can teach them to connect listening to and hearing what their body communicates to them, so they can stay embodied as they grow up. Being embodied is a natural state for children and something we tend to gradually lose through puberty as we try to 'be like everyone else'.

Keeping in tune with our body and connected with our intuition will protect us as life, school, friends, the media, and numerous other influences seek, inadvertently, to disconnect us from our true selves. If we are really honest with ourselves we can feel how 'life' teaches us to separate our minds from our bodies, how media or toxic people and other influences undermine our self-esteem and mean to harm us. As our children grow we can help keep them 'in tune' and connected to themselves so they can actually feel, and fight against, the toxicity of society. A large part of the benefits of encouraging and supporting curiosity in children is boosting their immunity against the ravages of the social world.

As our little child grow's we can teach them to respond to their senses and the messages their body gives them in the moment-to-moment: helping them to read the signs and signals accordingly. For example, when they appear to be feeling safe, secure, and are enjoying things ask them about how they feel. Ask them what do they think or experience in this moment? Or, when they seem 'frozen' ask them "What is your body telling you"? Do they sense that something feels strange or someone is unsafe? Teach them to trust what their body tells them. As they are getting older and can follow instructions, teach them to follow the 3 steps to keep themselves safer by **Saying No, Getting Away, and Telling an Adult they Trust**, anytime they feel that someone or something seems strange or uncomfortable to them.

As we explore the world of the senses with our children it can give us fresh eyes in to what it takes to be fully embodied and secure with ourselves and the environments we surround ourselves with. Because our sexuality is connected with our senses – our sensuality – becoming more embodied helps us to be more in tune with enjoying the pleasures of life. Pleasure and happiness is good for us and good for our children. Let's enjoy the ride and teach them to as well.

BBD Step 3: Encouraging Curiosity and Delight

Ages Birth to One

It feels easy to *Encourage Curiosity and Delight* at this age because everything that literally comes out of our baby is met with love (or at least keen interest). There is very little we don't consider adorable as our bond with them develops. Babies are designed to experience joy and delight from being with their caregivers, and research says that 'mutual joy is the basis for increased brain growth' (Circle of Security http://circleofsecurity.net). We delight in our babies under a year of age and encourage them to explore themselves, and others, with a gentle hand and heart.

Attachment in the 1st year

While baby grows within the mother's womb, neural pathways begin to develop through the senses, including those of attachment. As described in *Step 1: Talking About Bodies,* our newborn relies heavily on connecting and attaching through touch and other senses, finding comfort in the sounds of familiar voices, smells, and later, images. Whether birth was calm and peaceful, ecstatic, or traumatic, our babies are born with heightened sensitivity and sensuality because this is how they connect with and attach to the world around them. Once born, attachment pathways deepen almost wholly through the senses (Gordon Neufeld http://neufeldinstitute.org/).

We begin to model curiosity and, of course, find significant and meaningful delight from the moment we see, smell, or feel our baby. Infants detect our happiness and delight in them and this is the beginning of the secure attachment that every one of us needs to be whole, healthy and happy in these early years. There is much research done in this area so please explore. The Neufeld Institute http://neufeldinstitute.org/ is a great resource on parenting and the book *Rest Play Grow, Making Sense of Your Preschooler*, is a life changing one well worth reading.

The Circle of Security http://circleofsecurity.net/resources also has amazing resources to help support our parenting from birth on. It describes the importance of encouraging curiosity and delight, and step-by-step how to do that. It is a powerful resource that speaks about being a secure base our children can feel supported by when exploring things they are interested in, and how profound an affect this can have on their self-worth and confidence.

The Flow of Curiosity and Delight
In the first year of life the flow of curiosity and delight between parent and baby happens naturally, in both directions. For increased benefit to both, we can choose to bring more awareness and almost a meditation as we delight in our baby and their bodies.

This is the practice that begins it all – sensual communication. A large part of this sacred type of communication practice will focus on building comfort and bonding of both child and parent. Our children follow us with their curiosity and attachment as we guide them on the pathway to communicating their desires, needs, and boundaries. As they develop in this way so does their healthy self-esteem - and eventually healthy sexual self-esteem.

Part of the sensual communication practice in *Step 3: Encourage Curiosity and Delight* is paying attention to and responding appropriately to your baby's cues. It matters that their eye contact, face expressions, body movements, and other sounds communicate something. They will respond in some way to your touch and words, always, as their expression is at the most basic function of being human – they can hide nothing. We begin to recognize their cues as we 'read' them and respond accordingly, creating a greater bond and deepening of trust the more attuned we can be. Unlike what the last generations were told to believe, we cannot spoil a baby by responding 'too much' or 'too quickly'.

Reading their cues takes practice and awareness. At times they may seem to pull away, or look away, and this is a cue to stop or slow down whatever we are doing. We can watch them and tune in for a moment to see if they just needed a break or want to stop all together. Responding to their needs as quickly and as best we can helps our baby grow to become securely attached. It also teaches them to understand the foundation of communication – back and forth reading and responding. We don't have to get it 'right' much of the time. It is in our effort that our children understand how we love and care for them. Our efforts are rewarded though, as children who have a secure attachment are less demanding and more self-reliant as they grow up, making our job easier. It begins with reading and responding to their cues with the compassion and sensitivity we have, already, within our hearts.

Our baby's giggles, breathing patterns, smiles or other communications of enjoyment will let us know they are delighting in what we are doing as much as we may be. Playful touch encourages happiness as our baby experiences us enjoying them. They can read that we love being with them and this experience of our love is a building block of their self-worth. Giving our baby lots of cuddles and holding them as much as they want or need to be held (usually more than we can manage!) not only gives them pleasure and comfort, it fills their cup of wholeness.

Even at this tender age babies have a need for their adults to help them with their feelings and experience of the world around them. Holding them, attuning and responding to their needs, and playing with them in a tender, loving way all builds their ability to take pleasure in – and to trust - the world around them. Eventually we become a master at being able to read our baby and respond to them accordingly. We will discover that this important skill develops during sensual communication experiences.

Simple Examples:

"I am looking into your eyes and feel you want to play / sleep / eat"

"Are you feeling (fill in the blank)?"

"I can sense you are loving the way I am touching you."

"I am massaging your legs. Does that feel nice?" (Taking deep relaxing breaths will slow theirs as well and help them to relax in to our touch. Their mirror neurons will automatically make them take deeper breaths and sighs as well, just watch. ☺)

"Daddy loves cuddling you. You smell so good."

"Mummy loves the feel of your skin. Does that feel nice when I rub your back / touch your tummy like that?"

"I love your sweet little feet. When Auntie rubs your toes like this, does that feel good?"

As your infant approaches their first birthday they may begin reaching for, squeezing, or digging into their genital area. While using 'body science' terminology you can say in soft tones:

"Yes, that is your vulva/penis/scrotum/etc. It is good to touch it gently."

"It feels nice to touch your genitals/penis/vulva, doesn't it?"

"Nice and gentle when we touch …."

"Mummy touches your genitals when I wash them or when I need to look at them to see if you are healthy and clean. I will be gentle."

"Daddy is cleaning all the poo off your testicles / out of your vulva."(practice, practice, practice!)

BBD Step 3: Encouraging Curiosity and Delight

Ages One to Two

The second year of life brings growing curiosity and delight. As we bath, diaper, and change our baby our use of scientific terms for their private parts creates a repetition that encourages a natural and normal feeling for these terms. Along with practicing our use of scientific terminology, our gentle touch on our baby's body parts will help to create a sense of bonding and trust. Responding to our baby's cues when we touch them/ dress them/ clean them helps to build that bond and trust. Using soft tones of voice will help both parent and baby attune to the sacred and special moments that are being shared in our sensual / body communication.

Experiences of delight and trust in feeling and talking about the sensuality of our baby's body builds the foundation for them to learn to tune in to and communicate what they need, what feels right and what 'bad touch' might be like. There is a level of protection training even in this second year.

Supporting Their Exploration

As mentioned in *Step 2, Teach Boundaries and Consent*, babies and toddlers will naturally discover and want to explore and play with their genitals. Some start before their first year while others don't take much interest until their second year or later. Touching one's genitals at this age is generally done through the lens of curiosity and comfort. It may develop into a regular activity they do to comfort themselves and so they may resort to it more frequently than we'd like. If it makes us uncomfortable when they do this, we can gently say "Please do that in private" and move them to that area if they don't go there on their own, or stop the behavior and redirect them to something else in a casual way. If they are doing it in public/around others it will be important to reinforce firm boundaries, such as "Touching our genitals is something we do in the bath; in our bedroom, in private."

To protect their developing self-esteem it is important to try to support their curiosity, and follow their lead, whenever possible. As explained thoroughly in the *Circle of Security* literature, this builds their sense of security and attachment – that we are on their team and this makes our job easier. Think about when our child wants to play with something we don't necessarily like – sand, for example. Giving them an opportunity to do this in a place we are more comfortable, such as a sand table at a play centre, allows them to enrich their experience of life but keeps their exploration within a realm we can live with.

When we follow their lead and support their exploration it helps them feel as if we are 'on their side', building their trust in us. The same goes for genital exploration. If, at an appropriate time and place they want to explore their genitals, we can support this for them. As long as they have clean hands, are being gentle with themselves, and understand the boundaries of where and when, all is well. If we are uncomfortable it is easy to redirect them at this age and give them opportunities when we feel the activity is appropriate (on the change table or in the bath, for example).

As our children learn that touching their genitals is pleasurable they may want to do it more and more. It is a natural and normal practice but, of course, everyone feels differently about this. We can decide for our children what we believe is appropriate (and if we allow it at all), but if there is only one thing we **can** teach them about self-pleasuring/exploration is that they do it in private. 'In private' means by themselves in a place where no one else is, such as their bedroom, with no one else watching. This most basic foundation of supporting their exploration will help them reduce or eliminate shame about this natural human activity.

We can continue sensual communication exercises at this age through massage and when we are soaping them in the bath. Using gentle tones and a smile on our face supports our communication to mean one of pleasure and safety. 'Good touch' is something we continue to teach and model to our children through bathing, massaging, cuddling, and other affection.

Family Traditions

Making up games such as a family tradition of having a 'tickle talk' every Saturday afternoon can bring other experiences of 'good touch' to our children. A 'tickle talk' is when we each take a turn tickling or touching each other in our own way and discuss or respond in turn. This is a chance for us to model how to respond to touch we like or don't like. For example, when a parent doesn't like the touch or tickle our child chooses to do we express our feelings with words or sounds and maybe squirm away. When we like the tickle or touch our child has chosen to do we might sigh or giggle in pleasure. This can be a wonderful and playful way to teach about types of touch and boundaries on their journey to being a great communicator.

My first child was quite verbal and could speak in three word sentences by the age of 1. She learned the body science words and used them even at this age, which helped us to care for her better. I also practiced baby massage and had time to continue this when she was a toddler (and a lot more squirmy!). By the age of 2 she would sometimes ask me to massage or touch her: "Mummy tickle me?" I knew she meant touch her back in that 'special way' or run my fingers up and down her legs just the way she liked. Her ability to tune in to pleasure and be able to ask for it was positive thing, in my opinion. Our bond and her trust grew and grew over the years. As her mobility increased she would came over to me and ask "Mummy want massage?" It came as a beautiful surprise to me how we developed a nice give-and-take of massage and touch that we both enjoyed very much.

At almost 8 years old she still crawls into my lap and squeezes me, breaths in my scent, and sometimes even asks for massage or gentle 'tickle touching'. It is such a special bonding time between us. Because I encouraged her to sigh and breathe deeply when I massaged her at an early age she has grown up to do this automatically. Today she seems very comfortable in her body and without shame when it comes to enjoying herself. What a foundation for her future ability to give and receive pleasurable touch!

I continued a variation of this 'accidental tradition' with our second daughter and, later, our son. With my second I didn't feel I had the peace (or time!) to do much baby massage, and because I didn't start early enough I believe it became a bit of a foreign thing to us both. I came to realize we were missing a pretty important part of our bonding so have worked to increase our comfort with sensual communication. I began the tradition of the 'Tickle Talk' into our lives, bath her 1-on-1 when I can, and spend time cuddling her more while we read or watch media. Her body awareness and ability to communicate her wants and needs is improving as I focus on sensual communication with her. Every child is different, of course, but I believe this ability to know oneself, be embodied, and be able to ask for what we need, or state what we don't like, is a crucial life skill.

We have made a concerted effort to do sensual communication with our son, learning our lesson with our middle child. As our son approaches the age of two, he often climbs in to one of our laps and asks for "Touch! Again!" We play sweet little games of touching, massaging and tickling which is unique only to us. Often his sisters get involved and the communication deepens between us all as we give them boundaries of 'gentle' and 'listen to his no'. 'Stop immediately when anyone says no'. Sometimes we make a game of it to see how fast we can stop doing something when someone says no – this is not an easy skill to develop for children!

I deeply believe that the experience our children have of good, safe touch in a trusting, loving environment has given them all a certain special confidence. It has also broadened their knowledge and their ability to differentiate what is wanted or unwanted touch and when boundaries are crossed and how to best handle that. I often hear them telling each other "NO!" and "Don't do that!" or "That hurts!" This reassures me that they will be **more able** to protect themselves when it isn't just their sibling crossing their boundary.

Two Loops of Arousal

When our toddler or child touches our genitals, within the boundaries of their natural curiosity and our own comfort, we may get an erection and may feel embarrassed. A situation like this provides an opportunity for teaching our little ones about erections, to work on our ability to make things like erections matter-of-fact - if you can use the opportunity as a positive, shame free teachable moment to talk about body science. Remember, kids under 5 are very easy to teach about sexuality and body science. They are naturally curious about everything and have very little, if any, shame about bodies. If we can't find it in ourselves to talk about erections when they happen, smiling and saying something like "Interesting, huh?" will help keep things light.

As was discussed in *Step 2: Teach Boundaries and Consent*, erections can happen even if we don't want them to, and sometimes subconsciously, as in our dreams. This is due to the parasympathetic loop of arousal in our body/mind. https://www.ncbi.nlm.nih.gov/books/NBK11157/ Arousal is a *positive feedback loop* and so will continue to loop and increase until something stops it, like moving away from the touch or distracting oneself (or having an orgasm). During early childhood and especially in puberty, erections can just happen 'out of nowhere' and can also 'stop', or 'go down', on their own. We call these 'practice erections'.

A parent told me of a time when he was massaging his daughter's legs while watching TV and, to his surprise, found himself becoming erect because her foot was actually moving against his crotch area without notice. He stopped and moved her over a bit but then she asked for more massage so he chose to cover his genital area with a book and hoped she wouldn't notice anything. She didn't. I asked him what he would have done or said if she did notice? He said he would have probably shrugged and said something like: "It happens". I then gave this parent some coaching because if a child notices an erection and we choose not to say anything this teaches them that it's not okay to talk about it, potentially increasing body shame and secrecy. As well, if they notice an erection and we react and run off without saying anything this teaches *something* to our child. Being prepared with what we are going to say in these situations will give our children an opportunity to be curious, ask questions, and learn good habits of what is appropriate, where and why. A classic 'Teachable Moment'.

Simple Examples: <u>You can use examples from the previous age at any time.</u>

"You can see Daddy's penis is getting bigger. This is called an erection." "Boy's and Daddy's have erections even in their sleep to practice for making babies."

When dressing your child: "These are your nipples." "Does it tickle when Dad brushes over your nipples like that?" (smile)

When you find them fondling their genitals: "It feels nice to touch your penis/scrotum/vulva, doesn't it?" "It's good to be gentle." "Does it tickle/feel good when you touch your vulva? Does it feel nice?" This kind of communication helps them to describe how it feels so we can talk more about these sensations as they grow.

"Did you like the way grandma was cuddling you? Do you think it feels nice when someone we love and trust is holding us close?"

sensual education

ex) cream on genitals (tickles/feel good) Sensuality to body

BBD Step 3: Encouraging Curiosity and Delight

Ages Two to Three

The year between two and three is filled with wonder and curiosity about everything around our toddler. Many children this age are quite verbal as well, which makes everything easier and reduces the tantrum factor. Encouraging their curiosity in the world takes some courage as they are still so young and are a potential danger to themselves and others! Toddlers and preschoolers need a lot of direction and distraction to keep them safe while exploring their world. Boundaries and consent are an important part of what we teach at this age but keeping the guilt and shame out of their explorations can be challenging. On the up-side, most parents and caregivers typically find this age to be as delightful as the last.

Helping our toddler to safely explore their body without shame or guilt is empowering as well as protective. It teaches them to recognize and enjoy good and gentle touch, as well as what is uncomfortable, painful, or 'bad touch'. Along with teaching children how to safely and gently explore their body (and about the privacy of other's bodies), it is crucial that we help them to incorporate 'who, what, where and when' through boundaries and consent. Within this type of 'sensual education' please refer to and teach about *Step 2*.

As our toddler wants to explore their genitals more thoroughly we can direct them to be gentle, wash their hands before and after, and point out their body parts to them. Toileting may also come in to play at this point and with this stage comes much curiosity about the systems of the body. If we haven't already experienced them being very interested in our toileting we may see more of this type of curiosity now. Here again, it is important to recognize where our boundaries lie and to strengthen our ability to communicate them, without adding in shame or instilling guilt for being curious. Being curious is very natural. It is how we address their curiosity that makes all the difference to this age group. See the examples for ways to put our boundaries forward, to help them to have good boundaries while encouraging their curiosity, and to help them to delight in themselves and others.

Self-Pleasuring

Children are self-pleasuring from the time they are babies and toddlers. At this age it is generally curiosity and comfort that directs their attention to their genitals. As they grow, they may choose to do it more frequently, and more for pleasure rather than comfort. It helps parents and professionals to know this, and to know what to say and do in order to reduce shame about a natural exploration and comforting activity in our little ones. Similar to other private activities, there is a time and place for self-pleasuring.

Our little ones will benefit if they know this simply and matter-of-factly.

There are very few resources available that discusses or supports parents around their child's self-pleasuring activity (I prefer this term over 'masturbation'). None of what I found was really appropriate for children under 5. This is not surprising considering the amount of taboo, fear, shame and secrecy there is about the subject in just about **every** society on the planet. I did find a specific description of self-pleasuring in a guidebook for young people: *It's Perfectly Normal*, by Robie H. Harris (pg.48). There is a gentle and simple explanation with images that are mild. You may find it supportive for a conversation about this topic with your child. *It's Perfectly Normal* is a book for 10 and up, but I recommend getting it before your child turns 7.

I tell parents in my workshops that, yes, when they are humping a stuffed animal before sleep or watching TV with their hands down their pants, this is self-pleasuring. As in other ways our children explore we can support them to do it appropriately and safely. If our girl child wants to see more of her genital area we can suggest she use a mirror and take a closer look. She may want to see the entrance to her vagina or urethra within her labia/vulva. She will better be able to see herself if she can squat over a larger mirror.

Boys can do the same if they want to see 'what's what' in this position.

Encouraging our children to explore and enjoy their bodies and natural curiosities will continue to build their self-esteem and confidence. These are some of the building blocks for what they need to take care of and enjoy their bodies as they get older. Supporting them is a gift that will affect much of their future lives - so we continue our hard work on letting go of our negativity or embarrassment. Continuing with our self-reflection is important as well, so we are passing on messages that will empower and protect our young ones as they mature and increase their interactions with the social world.

Sensual Communication
We can continue with our practice of sensual communication as they grow and develop. Pointing out the way things smell, taste, and feel gives us opportunities for some great teachable moments. "Don't you just love the way roses smell? (breathing deeply, sighing) I can feel how good they smell all the way to my toes!"

We can continue to point out how their intuition comes up for them in certain situations and with certain people. "You seem to be drawn to that boy. Why don't you go over and ask him to play." We can ask them if they want to be massaged or touched gently as a way to calm down in the evenings before sleep. We can use sensual language (see examples) so they grow their awareness and understanding about the sensuality of their body and their feelings of pleasure. Part of the key here is that pleasure and good feelings are ok to talk about and to enjoy.

Siblings and Cousins

By the age of three, siblings can be well into their exploration of the 'other'. In many sibling groups the younger one is often on the receiving end of this type of attention and touch. It is crucial to teach them (all) about boundaries and consent. I have witnessed seemingly 'innocent' enough examples of games played by my three children, like 'Doctor' or 'Animals'. We try hard to be aware and guide them matter-of-factly.

The girls sometimes act out sexual type movements like humping or hip twisting such as they see on music videos (and who knows where else). Sometimes they practice on each other. It becomes obvious to them that this feels good and they peel into laughter as they enthusiastically continue. It is embarrassing for me - I definitely feel awkward if I'm watching this behavior - but I use the chance to check in with myself about the innocent play they are really doing and what is the harm? (Sometimes this is when we have a talk about 'what is sexy'...). We do remind them to watch the others' movements and communications for any 'no', of course. We remind them that they must tune in for any verbal or non-verbal cues to stop the activity and not follow if they move away. I have experienced them doing this type of activity for a short time, giggling away and then stop. I take some deep breaths and reflect on how my feelings of awkwardness and embarrassment arise, all the while smiling and nodding so they don't read my shadows!

In our family, sometimes their play includes some boundary crossing and I always stick up for the one who is saying 'no'. We are also very clear with them that our youngest, only 2, can't 'consent' to any type of genital touch or exploration from his sisters so they must only do that when a parent is around. Of course, our son needs to have an enthusiastic 'yes' to any requests to be touched, and we keep it brief and light. We also take the time to remind him to always tell Mum or Dad if anything happens to him that he doesn't like. There are often comparisons to what Mum and Dad have and these teachable moments usually include us bringing out a resource with other images of bodies so they can all see how different we all are.

If my sibling group included an older boy and younger girl I would be much more diligent about any kind of sensual play between them. I would recommend explaining that the boy typically has more power in these types of situations because he has a penis. When erect, a penis can hurt another person if used without consent. I would remind them that whoever says 'no' always rules and generally keep a close eye as they get older.

Why do I bring this up between the ages of two and three? Because I have countless stories from my parent education workshops where a parent opens up to the group about their sexual abuse or harassment that they sustained from their older siblings and cousins. Generally this happened when they were three or four (or older). It is always a tragic tale for me to hear and something that I believe could have been avoided. Imagine if we were equipped with body science and language, and the rules of boundaries and consent, how different our lives might have been? We must do this for our children, along with giving them the understanding that, even though things feel good, it doesn't mean you do them whenever you want and to whomever you want.

If this kind of thing has happened to you I encourage you, with all my heart, to find support to release your traumas and be on a path of healing. There are professionals who are just excellent at holding space and helping survivors like yourself to heal and move on. I wish the deepest courage and clarity for you if this is something you choose to do.

Simple Examples: We can use examples from the previous age at any time.
"It feels good to touch our genitals, doesn't it? It is important to have clean hands and to be gentle when we do this."
"Hugging and cuddling feels really good to me. Do you like it?"
"Do you like to be naked? I really like it and I am so happy that you feel good being naked too."
"Do you like being naked? I don't feel as comfortable as you but I am happy that you like it. Enjoy!"
"Mummy smells good, huh? It is so special to enjoy someone's smell. Take a deep breath."
"Doesn't that taste delicious? It is so pleasurable to enjoy how good something tastes. How do you feel?"
"I love the feeling of this soft blanket on my bare skin. How do you feel?"
"I see that you are exploring your genitals." "I am glad you are learning about your body." ("Did you wash your hands"? or be the judge how clean they are at that time and give gentle reminders about germs in our privates, if necessary). "Mummy will give you some privacy so you can enjoy this time with yourself. Let me know when you are done and we can wash your hands together".

BBD Step 3: Encouraging Curiosity and Delight

Ages Three to Four

Please review the section above as it pertains to this age and stage as well. Incorporate all the learnings about older siblings and cousins.

Acting out the Media

Between the ages of three and four children increase their focus and interest in acting out what they see in media, and indeed the rest of the world around them. They may start to sing lyrics that seem far beyond their years and dance in a 'sexy way' to copy what they are seeing. Some parents find this quite adorable and laugh and delight in what they see. Some find it quite shocking and it can be somewhat of a wake-up call as to 'where did they get that from?' It is important to be aware of our preferences as to what, where and how we want our young children to behave. This includes exposure to societal influences and therefore how they may choose to sing and dance.

It is crucial to remind our children what is private and public as far as the language we use and the body movements we do (see *Step 2: Teach Boundaries and Consent*). It is a confusing area for many parents because we may not want our children exposed to sexy type media but it is coming from everything around them – TV, movies and the internet being central. Beyond the obvious, there are more insidious modes of influence on a child's gender and sexuality, such as ads on public transit, what is in toy stores, and things coming from their peers. Have more complex conversations at this age about what is appropriate behaviour, within your value system. They will not be able to understand all the complexities at this age but the practice for us as parents and caregivers is invaluable. If we have been laying the groundwork and using language that supports teaching our children about the messages around them, we may find these conversations easier than we think.

It can be a delight watching our children as they dance and sing while encouraging their exploration in to what is 'cool' on the media in their lives. When we see our child using sexy type dance moves and singing lyrics that might seem too old for their age we can use these as teachable moments. We may take them aside and speak privately: "Honey, I really enjoy watching you dance that way and hearing you sing the latest pop songs but remember it is a 'sexy dance' and the words are about grown up things (like dating and sex). I think it's a better idea to do this type of thing at home and in front of people who know us. Feel free to sing and dance however you like in private!" This type of education will help our children to differentiate the what, where, and when of sensual or sexual activities and communications. It is empowering to be 'in the know' and to be self-aware.

Playing Doctor

Sensual and genital focused play and exploration begins to pick up as our child reaches their fourth and fifth year. Up to age three we may not have seen this type of curiosity and play but we may soon. They may have friends who are instigators and our children the happy recipients (we hope) of this type of attention and direction. These types of activities may be happening on playdates at the instigators house, with the parents being completely unaware. Most curiosity and play around bodies begins with someone of the same sex. Most of the stories I hear are usually 'wanted' by both parties, and games such as 'playing doctor' seems to remain a classic way that children act out genitally-focused scenarios.

Again, it will be important to review *Step 2: Boundaries and Consent* and ensure our child understands these important concepts. If they are engaging in exploring others bodies and we've done all our checks for appropriateness and safety, we may want to give them their privacy! This sends a strong message that we trust them and are supporting them to enjoy themselves as we would in other activities. This guides them to understand that well-structured and consensual play is okay to do. Being strong about giving them privacy also helps us when we would like to have some private time. Our children will be more likely to leave us alone when we request it. Great modelling helps our children become the kind of people we want them to become.

Simple Examples: <u>We can use examples from the previous age at any time.</u>
"Dancing sure feels good, doesn't it? I love to move my body too!"
"That singer is dancing in a sexy way. Do you see how she is moving her body? I can see how you are doing that too. Does it feel good to move like that? People like to dance like this because it feels good."
"People dance like this because it is sexy and attractive to others. Do you understand what that means?"
"Daddy loves to bath your beautiful skin (girl or boy). It is so soft. Am I being gentle enough when I wash you?"
"Cuddling you feels really nice. I'm so glad when we get to have this close time together."
"Mmmm. I love the smell of your skin."
"That person is so beautiful. I really enjoy watching them."
"You seem to be very interested in that boy. Do you like the way he looks or moves?"
Bodies:

"Do you like touching my/Mummy's breasts? They are very soft, aren't they?" (By three and up encourage them to always ask before they touch).

"How does it feel when I'm massaging you like this?"

"Let's be very gentle when we touch ourselves, ok?"

BBD Step 3: Encouraging Curiosity and Delight

Ages Four to Five

Our 4 to 5-year-old child is definitely tuning in to the media, their peers, and their body image by this age – for better or for worse. Some may be entering kindergarten and seem quite obsessed with what everyone is wearing, what music they like, and having friends. Others will still be in the position of not caring how they look and this can be easier on parents as we transition to this age of expansion into the social world.

Body Image and Self-Esteem

Positive encouragement of what our child's body can do, no matter how it looks, is paramount to a good body image. We can talk to them about how healthy or strong their body is. We teach our children that everyone is individual in every way from the other. If our child is focused on body image, how they look, how they move and what others think of them, our job may be a bit more difficult. It is important to follow their lead so that they can feel secure in our care - being able to trust that we believe what they want and like matters. We want to show them what's important about themselves and their relationships as well as what they need to reflect on and perhaps change their mind about. There are some excellent books and web resources available on how to build our child's self-esteem, on fighting negative body image, and on other social/emotional education. It is really important not to ignore the signs of a child who has an unhealthy body image and hope they go away or get better on their own.

Our child expresses their sensuality and individuality through the way they dress, their movement, the way they choose to dance and sing, and through their relationships. Enjoying and delighting in our growing child's expressions of their sensuality is a potentially beautiful thing. It may also be stressful on us as we feel they are growing up far too fast - we may feel out of control. While we have maximum influence on our children, under 5, it is crucial to educate them that how they dress and how they move communicates. How we choose to do this is up to us but take into consideration our filters and biases and reflect on how these inform what we say and how we say it. With three young children in my care I can tell you it is a constant work in progress!

Celebrate the Wonders of your Body

Encouraging our child's blooming sexuality takes courage and forethought. I love this one book gifted to my middle child, when she turned 1, by a dear friend of mine who is also a nurse. It is called *Beautiful Girl. Celebrating the Wonders of your Body* and is written by a female doctor. My friends' blessing inside reads: "Dear Lily, Happy 1st Birthday, beautiful girl. May you be brave and blessed". My friend was right: it takes a lot of bravery to be a girl in this world, a different kind of bravery to be a boy, and many skills and abilities for both to muddle through and thrive. The doctor who wrote this book spent her career helping women have a positive attitude about their bodies. It starts at a very young age. My wish is that by five years old the foundation of our child feeling solid in loving their bodies and feeling good and safe in the world is set. This is not an easy nor a simple task, especially if we ourselves suffer from body image and self-esteem issues. I encourage you to seek support and find freedom from these shackles that bind so many of us.

As we celebrate the wonders of our bodies and help and encourage our children to do the same for themselves, we can teach about the beauty and attraction we feel in things around us. Sometimes this can be as simple as saying "Daddy loves the smell of these beautiful flowers. Which ones do you like?", or, "I really like how that singer dresses and dances! What's your favourite (fill in the blank)?" When I experience one of my children stopping in their tracks as they watch something or someone they are attracted to, I usually put my arm around them so they know I am there and I support them in their wonder. There are usually no words shared but sometimes just a look which I return with a smile and / or nod. I believe this communicates a lot and, at the very least, my support in their expression and feelings.

Modelling our Sensuality and our Privacy

In my practice, during workshops, and often in private conversations on the side of a gathering, or on a school ground, conversations with parents sometimes goes to "How do you show affection for your partner in front of your children?" or more often "What do you do/say if you are 'caught'?" I believe it is a good thing to teach our children how to be in relationship and, for me, this includes physical affection with my partner.

I am sure I am not alone in saying how exhausted we feel and how little energy we have once the kids are in bed and the house is somewhat ready for the next day. I try to combat the inevitable separateness I experience with my partner by having 'private moments' in the middle of the busyness of our home life. We have extended hugs, gaze into each other's eyes, use whispered voices, and sometimes even kiss! ☺ The children usually notice and often run to join in on the fun (sound familiar?). Sometimes they don't notice, or don't care, and we can have a more private and deeper connection point. I believe this is great modelling of intimate connection that will make a difference for our children in their future relationships.

In the case of being discovered in more of a lovers embrace, I like to stay matter-of-fact and gently put up a boundary. If they ask "What are you doing?" I might say "We are having some private adult time right now. Get back to bed." Or "We'll be out soon". If they ask deeper questions we can always revert to the standard "That's a great question! Let's discuss that when we have our bath tonight, okay?" This gives us some time to consider how we want to answer their questions. We can also continue doing what we were doing before being interrupted, if we think it's appropriate. Taking care of our primary relationship is a good idea and is also good modelling for our children. Privacy is an important value. The key point here is to reduce any reaction so that the element of shame is kept out of the picture about what we are sharing with our partner. Celebrating our pleasures of life models to them that they too can take pleasure in the affections of their loved ones. We communicate that it is okay to feel good being intimate with others, when appropriate.

Self-pleasuring

Please review the self-pleasuring section in Ages Two to Three, above, as it pertains to this age and stage as well. It will be important to incorporate all the learnings about older siblings and cousins, also.

Generally a child aged four to five will naturally become more private about self-pleasuring and we may not see them engaging in this behaviour. If your child chooses to self-pleasure or comfort themselves in this way in public, in front of people in the home, or with their siblings, we need to correct the behaviour. There are currently very few resources to assist parents in this task but I did find one set with potential called *What Ellie Likes or What Tom Likes.* If you decide to purchase these resource(s) please ensure your child is at least 5 and has seen pictures of grown bodies and erect penises. I contacted the author and had a discussion with her about the choice of language (very limited), lack of body hair, and the size of the erect penis on the boy (huge). She let me know it was written for pre-pubescent children with intellectual or development disabilities so the concepts needed to be very basic, very simplistic, and that:

> "None of the books are designed to be used in isolation, without support of an understanding adult and in the context of wider learning about sexuality." Kate E. Reynolds, personal communication, January 2017.

In my experience, *What Ellie Likes/Tom Likes* are the first of their kind and can be helpful if we have a child who is quite active in their self-pleasuring activity, or struggles to have good boundaries.

Although incomplete in some ways these books provide clear communication concepts about healthy self-pleasuring. They demonstrate healthy boundaries, what is public and private, and healthy physical and emotional behaviours for **during** and **after** the activity.

It is also important to talk about healthy self-pleasuring with our children because some ways that a child chooses to explore can be risky and potentially damaging to the body (you can imagine some of the stories I've heard!). This makes sense because, as would be a natural occurrence in any other type of play, children experiment and much of learning is by 'trial and error'. Having a 'trial and error' experience with self-pleasuring, however, could turn in to a visit to the doctor.

We can also read up on some resources meant for older children to help guide our discussions about self-pleasuring and see how we can apply the information to our child in an age-appropriate way. Never hesitate to seek professional help. There is no shame in needing help yourself!

Examples are more complex: As we know, the concepts in Ages Four to Five are more complex so the examples are not as simple! Feel free to incorporate the examples from the previous age at any time. I also offer examples throughout each sub section. Here are a few more:

"Our body is beautiful and everyone is different. It takes a rainbow of differences to make this wonderful world go around so be proud of what you have and what you are."

"You are a spirited being who Dad loves so much. Tell me, what is your favourite thing about the cuddles we have together?"

"Feel for your testicles inside your scrotum. They are very sensitive little ball shaped things, aren't they? This where sperm will be made someday and you can help make a baby if you want to."

"Your Mum's like to have private time together too. How about you go back to bed and let us enjoy ourselves alone right now?"

"Healthy self-pleasuring means we do it in private, have clean hands, and touch ourselves gently. It's best to use only our hands so let's put that toy away for now. Enjoy and let me know when you are done so we can wash your hands together."

"It is interesting to look at other people's genitals, isn't it? Maybe our sister won't mind if we look? Let's ask her in the bath tonight."

"When our friends want to show us their private parts, always check in with yourself that you feel like doing that, okay? Use your words and even if they show you, you don't have to show them. It can be fun though, right?"

Closing

It's been a wild ride so far, this raising children thing. Although there is no manual we definitely learn by others mistakes and others' wisdom, but mostly we learn by how we were parented, reflecting on what we'd like to pass on, or change, for the children in our care. I had a lot of fun writing a book that I wished I possessed and digested 8 years ago, when I was pregnant with my first.

Since that time, I've learned a lot about what it takes, on the ground, to raise a healthy, happy, socially strong and body confident child. I must admit, I was quite lost in those first 3 years, for 'what to do, when' to help my child have a great start to life. Elements of her attachment, sensuality, body health and safety, and her blooming sexuality underwent a bit of a 'hit and miss', as she extended more and more into the social world. These were the reasons I began producing this resource while I was pregnant with Lily, over 5 years ago. The kind of support this book provides for our children's journey is so necessary and has not been available in this form until now. I have found very little in birth preparation books nor books for parents with newborns and up to age 3 - anywhere. It's been my honour to produce this comprehensive resource aimed at supporting parents and professionals from the very start – to teach children how to have a positive outlook on their body, their sexuality, and to learn how to enjoy it with delight.

Our self-worth is paramount to getting the most out of life and to be truly happy and at peace. Attachment, security, self-esteem – these are all the big pieces that build our self-worth - and unfortunately their foundation is laid at the most vulnerable time of our lives, the years between birth and five. It is not our parents fault - nor their parent's fault - that we are where we are. We all do our best and work with what we have.

My goals in life are to support people to heal themselves, become empowered with their sexuality, and support the children in their care to build a strong foundation – all this while we attempt to keep our ethics up with technological advances. We can do this by teaching our children to navigate the ravages of the social world healthfully and with joy, by being their own best friend, and having the tools and heart to be strong and compassionate first.

I hope you have found this resource helpful for your journey as a parent or professional to guide you within some of the more challenging aspects of our teaching and learning. These places of privacy and secrecy need some light these days as the internet makes us all so transparent. I believe that the tides can be changed and you are doing this simply by reading this book! You will be surprised how our perspective changes when we learn a little about something important to us, and how naturally we practice - finding our own way to say, do and be.

Blessings. Enjoy!

_____

*If you are able, please write a review on Amazon (or other area you purchased it through).

You can also help me spread this critical message by writing a post and/or following me on FB:
https://www.facebook.com/JuliaSaunders.SLI

Follow me on:
https://twitter.com/Julia_Saunders?lang=en
https://www.facebook.com/juliasaunders.sexloveintelligence/?ref=br_rs

About the Author

Julia M. Saunders, BHE (CSiS), MEd
Director of Sex Love Intelligence Education Inc.

While doing my Human Ecology and Critical Studies in Sexuality undergrad at UBC, 18 years ago, and spending many years involved as a 'sexpert' in a weekly radio show, on film, and television, my focus moved to find the root of what was missing in our sexual health education system. This search brought me to study a Masters in Sex Education Curriculum where I came to know that the school system, and all of the teachers in the system, desperately need support to teach about bodies, boundaries, and sex education. There is **still** no teacher education of this kind for our teachers in Canada!

Knowing that it 'begins at home' I started my quest to find out just how to do that and of course, met and was mentored by Meg Hickling. Saleema Noon also mentored me and supported the early development of my work.

As a sex educator in the system, I knew we needed more of our kind so joined Options for Sexual Health as a curriculum specialist and, together, we developed and launched the Certification Program for Sexual Health Educators. I pushed the boundaries here, as I did in this book, and helped to develop a program that is the only one of its kind in Canada. It still successfully produces highly trained and very effective sex educators who are doing great work around the Province and across the Country.

I continued to spend time trying to change the system by developing teacher education and creating a highly advanced Grade 4-7 curriculum for the Yukon Government. My coaching practice grew as more and more people reached me for help with their sex and relationship struggles.

Then I had children and everything changed.

As well as coaching, my focus is now on parents and professionals who influence and care for very young children. I finally found the root of social change and am working it every day at home with my three little ones.

For almost 30 years I have been on a growth path to self-love. I have worked hard to become emotionally and mentally strong and **integrated** and during this journey I have sought and mastered multiple modalities for healing and human potential. As my growth strengthened my wish for others to have this type of peace and empowerment grew. I found a way to do that and became certified in the highest distillation of world-wide methods to bring to my coaching practice. My clients can experience rapid results and dissolve issues at their root, meaning **problems don't come back**.

Please be in touch with me. Julia@slieducation.com

Some Testimonials from my Clients:

Sahara Exodus, Cuenca, Azuay, Ecuador

"Julia: I am in awe of your amazing session! You are naturally gifted with a big heart, and with fully conscious presence you hold space so beautifully. You helped me come out of my shell, and work your many skills as an incredible Coach/Counsellor! I appreciated how you took me through a number of levels - to go deeper - to break new ground. Because of the nature of who you are and the work you've done on yourself, I felt comfortable to allow you to break through my walls, and somehow you made your way to my core! Your powerful healing session delved deep into issues I've been struggling with for a long time and dissolved them. I now feel lighter being OK with it all. With this new awareness there is a light at the end of the tunnel."

Eva R., Registered Nurse and Counsellor, Vancouver, BC

"I experienced a Trauma Release session with Julia and had some incredible results! I didn't even realize that there was so much anger attached to the grief related to the death of my best friend's son. The process allowed me to discharge the anger and finally feel all my sadness and love. I will be able now to move on in my grief and support my friend in her sorrow."

Kathy Bazinet, Mental Health Worker, Ottawa, ON

"With Julia's gifted coaching she supported me to move from a very negative place: my feelings of not being seen, of not being acknowledged or accepted were completely eliminated during this 90 min session! The feeling of 'being home' within myself, being in a blissful pure place was fully achieved. I am filled with deep, profound gratitude!"

Marie France Dayan, Real Estate Investor / Private Lender, Montreal, PQ

"Julia, you are an amazing coach with a huge heart and presence! I went through a beautiful and wonderful journey thanks to you, which I will bring out in to my life and increase the ease with which I live. Your great presence, energy and professionalism was impeccable."

R. Walters, Edmonton, AB

"As a result of going through a session with Julia, I feel more freedom and peace in my life, and was able to work through some very difficult issues and clear the charge I had around them. I highly recommend Julia if you have an area in your life where you feel stuck, or are struggling to gain freedom."

Little Woo, Vancouver, BC

"Thank you so much doing a session with me to help alleviate the energetic trauma that I sustained many years ago from a near-death experience. It was fascinating to experience this somatic healing technique - I'm sure you will help a lot of people! Deep blessings for your passionate devotion to the healing arts, Julia!"

Resources for Young Children and their Trusted Adults

Bodies and Feelings

Parent's Resources (and older kids)

It's So Amazing!, by Robie H. Harris, illustrated by Michael Emberley.

It's Perfectly Normal, by Robie H. Harris, illustrated by Michael Emberley. (for age 10 up)

Sex is a Funny Word: *A Book about Bodies, Feelings, and YOU*, by Cory Silverberg, illustrated by Fiona Smyth.

What Makes a Baby, by Cory Silverberg, illustrated by Fiona Smyth.

Children's Resources:

Amazing You! Getting Smart about Your Private Parts, by Dr. Gail Saltz, illustrated by Lynne A. Cravath.

Boys, Girls & Body Science, *A First Book About Facts of Life*, by Meg Hickling, illustrated by Kim La Fave.

Happy in our Skin, by Fran Manushkin, ill. By Lauren Tobia.

It's NOT the Stork!, by Robie H. Harris, illustrated by Michael Emberley.

The Bare Naked Book, by Kathy Stinson.

Who Has What? All About Girls' Bodies and Boys' Bodies, by Robie H. Harris.

Boundaries and Consent

Parents Resources and kids over 5

Stick Up For Yourself! Every Kids's Guide to Personal Power and Positive Self-Esteem, by L. Raphael and G. Kaufman.
No Means No!: *Teaching children about personal boundaries, respect and consent; empowering kids by respecting their choices and their right to say, 'No!',* by Janeen Sanders, ill. Cherie Zazaming.
Good Pictures, Bad Pictures: *Porn-Proofing Today's Young Kids*, by Kristen A Jenson, MA and Gail Poyner, PhD, illustrated by Debbie Fox, Glen Cove Press, 2016 **
This book is written for parents and professionals of children 7 and over but I believe it is a powerful tool for parents and professionals of all ages to arm themselves against the ravages of the social world, both on line and off. When my 6 year old daughter was exposed to hard-core pornography on a play date (via a parent's smartphone) it came as a real wake-up call that I had not prepared her for these types of occurrences – to her detriment. My 4 year old will be getting this education before she is old enough to spell, as this is a marker for when they can search on-line and be exposed to 'bad pictures'. Some children may experience even earlier exposure due to older siblings or families that leave their devices around to be played with. The best defense is education and preparation **before anything happens like exposure to pornography.

Children's Resources (under 5)

I Said No! *A Kid-to-Kid Guide to Keeping Private Parts Private,* by Zack and Kimberly King, designed and edited by Sue Rama.
My Body Belongs To Me: *A Book about Body Safety*, by Jill Starishevsky, ill. Angela Padron.
Not Everyone is Nice, *Helping Children Learn Caution with Strangers*, by Frederick Alimonti and Ann Tedesco, illustrated by Erik DePrince & Jessica Volinski.
Your Body Belongs to You, by Cornelia M. Spelman.

Love, Family, Gender and 'Difference'

Parent Resources for Attachment, Security and Growth

Neufeld Institute http://neufeldinstitute.org/ for all things attachment, including amazing courses like *Making Sense of Your Preschooler* (a life changer!)

Circle of Security http://circleofsecurity.net/ This website is a gold mine of information about attachment, what to do in times of crisis and trauma, and super effective parenting tips and wisdom. The courses are very valuable (and free in many parts of the world) and the concepts are simple to learn. It totally changed the way we approach our parenting and brought a lot of peace to our house in a very quick time frame.

Rest, Play, Grow *Making Sense of Your Preschooler (Or Anyone Who Acts Like One)*, by Deborah MacNamara, PhD. (Based on the relational developmental approach of Gordon Neufeld.)

Children's Resources and Stories

10,000 Dresses, Marcus Ewert, Rex Ray.

Asha's Mums, by Rosamund Elwin.

A Fire Engine for Ruthi, Leslea Newman, Cyd Moore.

All I Want to Be is Me, Phyllis Rothblatt.

Ballerino Nate, Kimberley Brubaker, R.W. Alley.

Daddy's Roomate, by Michael Willhoite.

Daddy, Papa, and ME, by Leslie Newman, Ill. By Carol Thompson.

Heather has Two Mommies, by Leslea Newman, Ill.'s Diana Souza, Dana Kingsbury.

How Would You Feel if Your Dad was Gay? By Ann Heron and M. Maran.

M is for Mustache, by Catherine Hernandez.

Made by Raffi, by Craig Pomranz, ill. By Margaret Chamberlain. **
Author: I wrote the book to support young boys and girls who are perceived as "different" because of their appearance or hobbies. It is a funny colorful book with a serious message and will interest those who care about promoting diversity and embracing our differences, as well as all children seeking to fit in.

Mommy, Mama, and Me, Leslea Newman, ill. Carol Thompson.

Max, The Stubborn Little Wolf, Marie-Odlie Judes, Bourre Martine.

My Princess Boy, Cheryl Kilodavis, Suzanne DeSimone.

Pearl Power, Mel Elliott.

The Different Dragon, by Jennifer Bryan.

While You Were Sleeping, by Stephanie Burks.

Parent's Resources

The Transgender Child, by Stephanie Brill and Rachel Pepper.
Gender Born, Gender Made: Raising Healthy Gender-Nonconforming Children, by Diane Ehrensaft.

Websites
genderspectrum.org
childrensnational.org
kidshealth.org
ourtruecolors.org
imatyfa.org
pflagcanada.ca

Encouraging Curiosity and Delight

Children's Resources

The Way I Feel by Janan Cain
Beautiful Girl, Celebrating the Wonders of Your Body by Christiane Northrup, M.D., illustrated by Aurelie Blanz.
I Wonder, by Annaka Harris, illustrated by John Rowe.   (A book that celebrates the feelings of awe and curiosity in children, as the foundation for all learning.)
Little Pleasures, by Elisabeth Brami.

Children over 6 years

Things Ellie Likes / Things Tom Likes, A book about sexuality and masturbation for girls/boys and young women/men with autism and related conditions, by Kate E. Reynolds, illustrated by Jonathon Powell.

Parent Education Book for Older Kids and Teens

Talk Sex Today, by Saleema Noon and Meg Hickling.

Adults Only
Truthful Photographs and Stories about Bodies

The Bodies of Mothers: A Beautiful Body Project, by Jade Beall.

Bare Reality: 100 Women, Their Breasts, Their Stories, by Laura Dodsworth.

I'll Show You Mine, by Wrenna Robertson. ** This is a valuable book to own and depicts real images of women's genitals – front view and 'spread leg' view, with a personal storey, in her own words, about how she experiences herself as she is. In today's world, with growing numbers of women seeking to alter their genitals (labiaplasty) and constant digital alteration of photographs of vulva's, women, and men, are left with a very narrow view of what is real and natural for a woman. **This is a growing concern for young women today as they go through puberty**. I find this book even more valuable than *Petals*, as it is in colour (not sepia) and has the two angles/view points of the vulva as well as the every important personal storey of empowerment.

Petals, by Nick Karras. ** This book is a picture book of women's vulvas, generally in a slightly aroused state. As these images are rare to find in society I felt this parent support guidebook would be a good place to advertise its availability. It is compiled to help women and men to experience the wide variety of vulvas in a safe way that is not pornographic. It is a book used by doctors today to aid women who have body issues about their labia, to help them make the best decision for themselves if they want to get labiaplasty (surgery) to reduce their labia minora.

This Is Who I Am: Our Beauty in All Shapes and Sizes by Rosanne Olson.

Understanding Body Dissatisfaction in Men, Women and Children, by Sarah Grogan.

The End (But really, just the beginning!)

Additional Notes:

Made in the USA
Columbia, SC
26 May 2017